"Staying happy, healthy and balanced is critical to perform at the highest level. No matter what your endeavor, if you're burned out, distracted and overwhelmed you're going to be leaving results on the table. In Digital Detox Secrets Lisa shows you how to avoid that increasingly easy to fall into trap. She brings a supremely practical approach to achieving work-life balance and maintaining a happy, high performing mind. Digital Detox Secrets will seriously serve anyone struggling to create the space needed in their lives to really live!"

— Rian Doris, Chief Growth Officer,
Flow Research Collective

"Surviving, let alone thriving, in a toxic digital world can be a struggle for even the savviest and intelligent of people. Thank you, Lisa Buyer, for the many insights on how to stay true to our core humanity and help us bring our whole selves into each day, each relationship, in this hyper-connected society that is the new normal of the digital age. I need to use my CBD oil now and do some yoga."

— Erin Fravel, Finance Executive, SAP

"Lisa Buyer has created a succinct and powerful guide to not just survive but thrive in the digital era. It's game-changing."

— Will Kleidon, Founder and CEO, Ojai Energetics

"Most entrepreneurs are so busy creating products and services to help others that they frequently ignore their own minds and bodies. Lisa shows how paying attention to yourself not only improves your life, it's also good for business!"

— David Meerman Scott, entrepreneur and *Wall Street Journal* bestselling author of eleven books including *Fanocracy*

"In a world that's speeding up, how do we slow down enough, to not just survive, but to thrive? I found the stories and the hacks that Lisa shares in her latest book, Digital Detox Secrets, excellent solutions. Both, in my personal journey, as well as our work in consulting for virtual teams, it is imperative to know how our minds are affected by the digital acceleration... Thanks Lisa, for succinctly giving us the tools to be our best selves in our evolving times."

— Anna Shilina, Human Behavior Specialist &
Founder of Akuna X

"If you are a parent, a smartphone addict or a marketing, PR, social media professional this book is a MUST-read. Lisa Buyer not only writes about digital detox, but she also lives it. While running her social PR agency and speaking at conferences she took her experiences of the always-on world and delivers actionable zen bytes of how to disconnect and still get things done."

— Navah Berg, Social XR Communications Professional

DIGITAL DETOX SECRETS

How to Create Space in Your
Life for Health, Happiness,
Opportunity, and Productivity

LISA BUYER

ISBN: 978-1-64184-168-9 (paperback)

Dedication

to my sister
Christi
we survived
and
thrived.

Acknowledgment

Thank you
Navah Berg for pushing me
Andy Duesnes and Sarah Collins for
creating space for me to finish
Londyn Swanson for artwork on the cover
Don, my husband, for the love and support

Table of Contents

Section 1
Lifestyle—Health, Wellness, and More

Section 2
Workstyle—Business and Productivity

Section 3
Socialstyle—Social Media, Selfies, and More

Foreword

The digital age, is it only a number or a choice?

As a doctor approaching the age of 60, I've learned a lot along the journey called *life* about what it takes to age well. One of my biggest takeaways has been understanding the importance of making healthy lifestyle choices in areas like nutrition, exercise, sleep, and *detoxification*.

Twenty years ago, I met an extraordinary marketing/public relations executive by the name of Lisa Buyer. My new endeavor required the qualifications of such an expert, and I credit Lisa with the huge success of the company I co-founded at a time when functional and integrative medicine was just bubbling up. I suppose that somewhere during the last two decades, I must have rubbed off on her (and as much as she changed me!) and she learned many of the lessons I often spoke about, including the need to detoxify.

In the field of detox, it never occurred to us until relatively recently that we needed to detoxify from our digital devices, computers, mobile phones, apps and all that social media we find glued to so much.

Truth be known, our simple human brain is capable, but not structured, of being constantly stimulated in the manner that a flashing screen, the compulsion of online games, the curiosity of every other person's personal life, the fear of missing out [#FOMO], and the non-relenting stream of misinformation.

Digital information has become a toxin on its own.

To understand my knowledge, experience and expertise, let me tell you a bit about myself.

Traumatic Trajectory

My life started in a small town located in Michigan. I was the more introverted and less athletic of twins — the youngest children in the family — I grew up shy, quiet, and alone. My friends were comic books. My adventures were in science fiction. Intelligence was my strength.

When I came out as gay at 15, my dad tried to drown me in a lake. I guess he thought I'd be better off dead than living as a "faggot" in the '70s. Off to college at 18, I spent a year begging my mom to let me come home. My parents felt I should stay to "fight my demons."

Eventually, fear of being on my own morphed into anger at being pushed away. I turned to alcohol, and my anger changed me. It fueled my need to study and learn — the only things I felt I could control. From medical school and residency through ten years in the ER, I saved every one I could. Meanwhile, I descended into alcoholism and depression.

Midlife Resurgence

When I looked up at 35 years old, I was a mess.

I had significant heart disease, high blood pressure, and borderline diabetes. I drank, smoked, wasn't sleeping, and weighed 265 pounds.

Finally, it hit me: **If I didn't change soon, I was going to die.**

I fixed my diet, learned about detoxification and supplements, started on testosterone, and practiced martial arts every day. And within 18 months, my body fat was under 15% for the first time in decades.

My emotions felt secure, my sleep returned, and strength surged through my body.

Eventually, I discovered the importance of balanced hormones. I used this knowledge to start a business and it took off, growing into a network of more than 50 centers practicing bioidentical hormone replacement therapy across the United States.

Something Missing

After four years of hard work, it all fell apart. I had to walk away from the business I co-founded with my twin brother ironically, with just a few dollars to show for it.

Fear, anger, and hurt returned.

I spiraled back into alcoholism. I started smoking again because it numbed the pain. My weight skyrocketed. And again, I was faced with my life-threatening friend called heart disease. I was in worse condition than ever.

From my previous go-around, I learned that I could change everything — for a little while.

Realization - I had failed to consider my soul, my heart, and my spirit.

I found a wonderful life coach who said something shocking. She told me I was one of the most ungrateful people she had ever met. I was stunned and confused. *What did she mean, ungrateful? Me?*

I had survived
my dad's attempt to drown me.
I had survived
my college years and become a doctor.
I had survived

the illness of my 30s.
I had survived
alcoholism.
I had survived
the loss of my business.
I had survived all this,
but I persisted in framing myself as a *victim*.
I saw all these events as failures
and not for what they were:
miracles.

Practicing Gratitude

My life coach taught me what was lacking in my previous attempt at health: simple gratitude. She prescribed action — an expression of appreciation — not a change in perspective. I didn't need to believe in the process; I just had to do it!

Today- every morning, after I walk the dogs and prepare for work, I sit in front of my computer and list everyone and everything I appreciate.

True health begins with gratitude.

Until I cleaned my emotional house — all the retained anger, fear, hurt, and sadness — I couldn't sustain the physical and mental portions.

Now, a decade has passed, and I'm not only grateful but healthy as well.

If you don't clean up your emotional toxins in your work, social and personal life, the rest won't hold for long.

Detoxification is a way of Life

As gratitude keeps the emotional toxins at bay, detoxification of the body should be an essential part of your daily routine.

The method of "toxins in, toxins out" needs to be performed as part of everyone's daily routine.

This book "Digital Detox Secrets" covers in length the importance of monitoring your food, environment, stressors, and emotional responses!

In addition, Lisa Buyer, the author of "Digital Detox Secrets" has been an expert, a strong proponent, and practitioner of detoxification bio-hacks for the past 20 years.

Our team at Forum Health has strongly relied upon Lisa to get the message out to the public (something which physicians often are not equipped to provide).

The purpose of this foreword is to get you, the reader, excited and interested in your health, your life, and your wellness. I hope that with my story, you can reflect on your life and come to understand (before life teaches you) that detoxification is the hidden secret to health!

In all health!

Dr. Paul Savage MD

Dr. Savage is co-chief medical officer of Forum Health's and its founding practice: Agenixs, a concierge anti-aging clinic. After more than 20 years in the field, he's nationally sought-after as a lecturer and consultant for his insight on regenerative medicine and hormone therapy.

He co-founded a physician network specializing in hormone therapy and worked with Lisa Buyer's agency in its branding and public relations — helping it grow to 50-plus locations.

Savage graduated from the University of Michigan School of Medicine. He is board-certified by the American Academy of Anti-Aging Medicine. He's also certified in integrative medicine through George Washington University.

Introduction

My friend Matt told me I had to write an introduction to Digital Detox Secrets explaining why I was qualified to write this book. The fact is, anyone can write a book on a topic they're passionate about and have experience in.

Having started my first business in college hand-painting T-shirts to pay the bills, I know what it's like to be in survival and scale mode. I watched my mother, a single mom with no financial support, struggle to raise two daughters on her own. She was always in a survival mode of her own.

Experience and Passion

Before I turned 25 years old I experienced being sexually abused as a teenager, a serial killer murdering two of my good friends in college, my boyfriend's father committing suicide, a close circle of friends being killed in a plane crash on the way to a Gator football game, finding an assisted living home for my elderly father, and his passing away.

Parallel to all of the tragedy and challenges by age 25, I also successfully made it into college and graduated with a degree in public relations from the University of Florida. I was in a happy relationship and got engaged. I chose my friends wisely and surrounded myself with the most successful and inspirational people and sources I could find. I started my own public relations agency at 24-years old and set up shop to be in control of my own destiny.

My life was good and, it is still good. Just not without breakdowns and breakthroughs.

The tragic experiences at an early age fractured me, my friends and my relationships beyond words. They also broke us down and made us put ourselves back together.

Breakups, marriages, divorces, kids all came with the territory.

Market crashes, backstabbing clients, dotcom highs and real estate lows were par for the entrepreneur landscape.

Although I suffered more on the personal side - my business scaled so successfully I attracted a partner to buy in, only to have the dot-com bomb a month later and many of our clients vanished in thin air.

Through the years I have reinvented myself and my business.

Why? One must reinvent in order to survive. Tony Robbins' 30 days success program in my twenties, thirties, and forties is how I reached my goals and followed my passion. I threw myself into all the self-help books, classes, and courses while also subscribing and investing in all the business mentorship I could find.

In retrospect - discovering yoga in my late twenties saved my life and empowered me to push through daily dramas and differentiate between stories and realities.

As soon as the digital revolution started with search engines and social media networks popping up I was *all in* -personally and professionally. My agency immediately transformed into weaving in Google, Facebook, Twitter, LinkedIn into the PR mix. Things have never been the same in so many positive and also destructive ways.

Today, digital, social media, smartphones, multiple screens are part of every business and everyone's lives no matter the generation or type of brand.

We live in a 24/7 world without timezones or boundaries. It comes at a price.

Gone are the days when it was cool for startups, entrepreneurs, and professionals to work long hours and stay at the office late. Investors want healthy teams with proactive well-being in mind.

But wait - what about those emails and notifications that never stop?

My first book Social PR Secrets, now in its 4th edition, is a business book about how to effectively mix social media and search marketing as part of the public relations cocktail. I've built a business around digital and digital has built a business around me.

Best and Worst

The #MeToo movement is one of my favorite moments - and movements - thanks to social media. Because, yeah, #MeToo. There is not one woman I know who does not have a #MeToo story.

One of my worst moments in digital was watching the "takedown" of my teenage daughter thanks to social media, smartphones, and FOMO. We are beyond it now, I talk in detail about this in several chapters.

Digital Detox Secrets is a curated version of all my personal and professional digital survival model tips, tricks, hacks stories and ways to create space in your digital life for health, happiness, and productivity. It took me almost five years to publish it, I've been *picking* at it and honestly felt insecure about it.

Writing a book is like coming out of the closet - it is scary, invigorating and freeing.

That voice - *what if I fail? What if someone calls me a fake?* I even got my 200-hour yoga certification as part of the "research and development" of this book. Little did I know it would be the best R+D for me personally.

I felt guilty not sharing this information with the world - if it helps one person create more space in their lives - that's the goal.

If you want to continue on the Digital Detox Secrets journey - check out the podcast and subscribe to the weekly magazine.

Who is this book for?

- Entrepreneurs

- Mompreneurs

- Intrapreneurs

- Digital Natives

- Digital Disruptors

- Parents, grandparents, aunts, uncles and teachers

- You

Fill in the blank with

This _____ does not define you.

Day
Event
Person
Post
Comment
Notification
Feeling
Mood
Word
Device
Chapter
Drink
Food

Disease
  Weight
Workout
  Email
Job
  Moment
does not define you.
Remember
Feelings are not facts.
Perception is not reality.

I wrote this book to be a collection of stories, interviews and tips to help you find balance in this digital world. Whether you are an entrepreneur, mompreneur, intrapreneur, parent, teenager - these are curated ways I have found to create more positive space in our lives.

Hit play or pause when you need it.

Section I

LIFESTYLE—
HEALTH, WELLNESS,
AND MORE

Reprogramming Mind, Body, and Spirit

HAVE YOU EXPERIENCED anxiety, depression, or severe panic attacks? Check. Have you been told it could be your smartphone, social media obsession, or the multiple screens in your life? Guilty.

Have you ever experienced body image issues? Maybe. Too many "plandids" or selfies and not enough candids. Who me? Do you have a difficult time finding your passion, what makes your heart smile and your soul sing? Let me check Facebook.

Is it our digital world, or has life always been this challenging?

I started interviewing people and started with Lisa Gianvito, a yoga and wellness coach, to find out how she guides people to a healthier, happier version of themselves.

When Gianvito started having panic attacks at age twenty-seven, she reluctantly turned to yoga and meditation thanks to doctor's orders. Even though she's a busy entrepreneur who owned a successful hair salon, she cherished her gym workouts. At the time, the words "yoga" and "meditation" did not exist in Gianvito's schedule or vocabulary. Little did she know, they were about to.

It seemed unfathomable that something as passive as meditation could be so beneficial. As an entrepreneur or mompreneur, every minute is precious, calculated, and measured on efficiency and productivity. Yoga and meditation don't seem to gel with our multi-tasking mentality. Slowing down, even stopping, seems counterproductive in this 24/7 digital world.

Reluctantly, Gianvito took her doctor's advice. After listening to a few meditation tapes, there was that *aha* moment when her mind actually stopped for a minute, and that feeling felt—well—good!

"I started listening to a guided meditation, and I quickly noticed that my mind wasn't racing, and my heart wasn't beating out of my chest. Then I added yoga videos (there were no yoga classes where I lived)," Gianvito said.

"It felt really good, and I began to see my body in a whole new light."

Like many people who try yoga and meditation, Gianvito wanted more. So much so that she went on to get her 200-hour yoga certification, then her 500-hour certification.

Fast forward to now, and Gianvito has sold the hair salon she owned for 25 years and traded her outer beauty skills for a business focusing on the inner beauty of wellness. Today, you can find Lisa as a mind, body, spirit coach offering doses of digital detox.

#DigitalDetoxSecrets

We are one and whole. Gianvito reminds us with her tips that we must focus on the mind, body, and spirit to make definite and positive changes in our lives.

Lemon Aid

Gianvito recommends waking up to warm water and a half of lemon. Start your day with a warm cup of water and add in half of a freshly squeezed lemon. The idea is to get rid of the acidity in the body, and although lemons seem acidic, they actually help reverse the acidity in your body to alkaline.

Lemon water helps your pH balance and triggers improved digestion, reduces heartburn, builds your immune system, contributes to weight loss, clears the skin, and speeds up the body's elimination process. Who knew one food could hold so many detox benefits?

Meditation Baby Steps

After you start detoxing your body, your mind is next. It can be intimidating to start working meditation into your daily schedule; especially when it feels like you are not really doing anything but sitting.

Gianvito recommends starting with an app such as InsightTimer. You can pick a mediation, from one minute to forty-vie minutes long, and you can customize your experiences such as mood, sound, and time.

InsightTimer offers special tracks on love, relationships, anxiety, sleep, and depression. You can even look at the advanced and upgraded options from the free version and join groups, take courses, and be part of a community of 5 million InsightTimer meditators.

Just Move

Forget the gym membership or waiting for a friend to go with you to a studio. Get up, get out, and walk outside. Pause the gym membership and save your money. Keep it simple and honor who you are. There are also tons of free videos on YouTube.

Positive Transformation Starts with Affirmation

The number one thing that helped Gianvito transform her life was positive affirmation. She uses positive affirmation when journaling and by repeating mantras over and over again in her head. This is called reprogramming your brain with positivity. Mantras should always be spoken and written in the present tense as if you already have or already are the thing you want.

I love myself.

I am happy.

I am strong.

I am compassionate.

Reprogramming your brain is possible. Even if you are on a treadmill, start repeating the affirmation. Soon, you will see things in a new light, and the negativity shifts and possibility begins.

Be Honest, Be Authentic

You can justify the shit out of your life, but that doesn't get you anywhere.

Be real, be honest, and make the commitment. Stop procrastinating.

If you really want to change, you will do it.

The reason you don't want change is that you don't want to do it!

The After-Party

Catch up with Gianvito if you want more. She offers digital detox programs, Skype coaching, and specialized yoga classes and events.

Follow her on Instagram and Facebook. @lisagianvito

···2···

Digital-Destress

A PSYCHOLOGIST PACED around the room as she spoke about managing stress to the audience.

She raised a glass of water. Everyone expected her to ask the question, "Is the glass half empty or half full?"

Instead, she smiled and asked, "How heavy is this glass of water?"

The audience's guesses ranged from four to eight ounces.

The actual weight has no real significance.

What does matter is how long I hold the glass.

If I hold it for a minute, it does not feel so heavy. If I hold it for an hour, my hand might start cramping up.

If I hold it for a whole day, my arm will probably become numb and feel paralyzed.

In each case, the glass's weight does not matter, but the longer I hold it, the heavier it gets.

What's the point?

Stress and anxiety are like a glass of water. If we stress about things for a short while, nothing happens.

If we think about them for a long time, they start to hurt.

If we think about them all day, we will feel paralyzed; unable to do anything.

It is important to remember to let go of whatever stressed you out.

So, every evening, as early as possible, put away the stress you have carried during the day.

Don't carry things throughout the evening and into the night.

Remember to put down your glass of water.

I found that story in my Facebook newsfeed one day and thought it was the perfect introduction to talking about how to eliminate the space we allow for stress in our lives.

What exactly is stress?

It's a state of mental or emotional strain or tension resulting from adverse or very demanding circumstances. That could be working too much, not getting enough sleep, worrying about things you can't control, focusing on negative thoughts, doing things for the wrong reasons, saying yes to everything, or eating the wrong foods.

A big stress factor for all of us is money: not making enough, having enough, or owing too much. That's why managing your money and living within your means is critical to your happiness and stress levels. The money is not causing the stress; it's the decisions you make around the money that adds up to high-stress levels.

Just one more email to read, Facebook post to write, Instagram like, and scroll.

How much stress do you carry each day?

It's like a badge of honor. In some crazy twisted reasoning, if we are not stressed, it's as if we don't care or that we are not working hard enough. Many equate stress to effort. The more stressed, the harder we must be trying. So, in some insane way, we think all that stress will pay off in huge dividends of success. We'll eventually make more money, have more time, get that job, earn that recognition, have that baby, or buy that boat. But then, that's just a new kind of stress.

Our lives are even more triggered with stress thanks to social media and the insta-world we live in. Stress can manifest and lead us down a path of slow self-destruction when it is combined with eating cupcakes, Oreos, and ice cream or drinking a ~~glass~~ bottle of wine. I guarantee that going to happy hour after work every night and the oh-so-easy solution of turning to prescription drugs for relief is not the answer.

Before you know it, you have stress *and* other problems such as being overweight, becoming addicted to drugs and alcohol, or making very poor decisions while under the influence.

Here's what happens to your body when stressed:

- Heart beats faster
- Blood pressure increases
- Breath becomes shallow and rapid
- Blood sugar rises
- Adrenaline and cortisol production surge
- Immune system weakens
- Production of sex hormones decreases
- Digestion is halted

How much stress do you let go of each day?

What's the first thing we do when feeling stressed? Eat, drink, and sleep. All seem like they should be part of our daily life, but too much or too little can lead to destruction.

Stories. We have so many stories happening in our head that never come true. The "What if...?" stories that lead us down to the depths of despair. *True Story: The brain can only handle one thought at a time. Focus on one thing at a time.*

Breath. Create space in your body for long, deep breaths. Remember to exhale the negative and inhale the positive. Shallow breathing promotes anxiety, depression, and panic attacks.

Energy. The more you move and activate, the less stress you will carry with you. Take 250 steps every hour and walk your way into a better day.

Being. How often do you give yourself even five minutes a day of silence? *Close. Your. Eyes. Shut. It. Down. Be.*

Letting go. Holding on to negativity breeds useless energy and depletes your ability to cope and think clear. *Remember, karma is always watching.*

Nutrition. Your body is your temple; nourish it with whole foods and stop eating the white stuff. *Organic, no sugar, green is good.*

Sleep. REM, light sleep, and deep sleep are all critical to rest, restore, and rejuvenate the body's hormones and brain functionality. *Track your sleep analytics with a Fitbit and set sleep goals.*

Smiling. Believe it or not, smiling comes out in your voice. We hide behind conference calls in our PJs and read our emails while listening. *Stop. Focus. Smile. It improves your immune system, mood, mindset, and perception.*

Posture. Sit up straight and open up space in your spine. You have seven different chakras in your spinal column from your crown chakra (brain) down to your root chakra. All the chakras relate to an organ or a gland. Sit up tall and open the chakra. *Want a natural high and mind reset? Try Kundalini yoga and discover breath of fire and more.*

Happy place. Find your happy place (besides the local bar) and go there often. It could be a cozy room in your house, a spa, or even the man cave or glamper.

Unschedule. Block out pockets of "me" time each day. Wake up an hour earlier, light a candle, pour a cup of coffee, and set up your day.

Friends and Family. Not all friends and family are healthy. Set boundaries and weed out the negativity. Surround yourself with people who bring you joy. *It's okay to disengage with friends and family who suck the life out of you.*

Gratitude. Things can change in a flash. Be grateful for the precious moments. *The words "thank you" are a superpower.*

Take a social media break. Disconnect periodically when it makes sense. Few expect you to be tethered to a device 24/7. Friendly reminder, you own your device, your device does not own you.

Digital Detox Secret

Tap into and out of stress. I'd never heard of tapping until I interviewed Karen Berzanski, Pro EFT Tapping coach and life coach who understands the digital stress of our daily lives and helps people overcome it, whether it's getting visibility as an entrepreneur or making the same mistakes over and over, stuck in an endless loop of self-sabotage.

"We're literally tapping on the meridian and points on our body," said Karen. "Tapping is a combination of ancient Chinese acupressure and modern psychology. And what we're doing when we're tapping, physiologically speaking, is we're turning off the body's fight or flight response."

The amygdala in our brain is our body's alarm center. When we feel triggered or activated in any way by either the little daily stressors in our life or by something that reminds us of something that happened in our lives when we were younger, that fight-or-flight center goes off.

Tapping sends a calming signal to our brain and tells our body that it's safe to calm down and relax, and it's safe to feel grounded at this moment. It takes us from what I call freaked-out brain into peace spring. When we're in freaked-out brain, we're all over the place, we're frazzled.

We unknowingly invite stress into our life when we fail to make a daily intention to create space each day to de-stress. Tap into your fears and reclaim space. It's important to have an environment that supports you the kind of mindset you really want to build for yourself.

Sometimes it's time to shine a flashlight on what is holding you back.

#DigitalDetoxSecrets
My daughter experienced some trauma three days before she was going to take her SAT test. I tapped into Bill Dovel RN, Pro EFT™ Master Practitioner, CPMP to help her reset. Here's what tapping can help:
Tapping on your body's super comforting points
Turning on the body's record button
Deleting the reactions you don't like
Programming in the reactions you want

The After-Party

Catch up with Karen or Bill if you want more. They offers digital detox programs and personal development.

Follow Karen on Instagram and Facebook. @karenberzanski

You can find Bill here http://www.proeftcenter.com/

•••3•••

Space for Yoga

LOCUST AND CORPSE poses are more than insects and dead bodies.

In the early start-up years of my agency, I found it hard to get to the gym, so I bought *Cindy Crawford's Shape Your Body* workout video to do sweat sessions in my living room. It was the era of the color-coded workout outfits and instructors with high-pitched sorority voices teaching step classes.

My Barbie doll tolerance level was low, and my fashion statement was not about wearing a thong leotard and white Reebok high tops. With her celebrity trainer Radu coaching, Cindy's video was a refreshing mix of workouts to shape your whole body from lightweights to lunges to Pilates and yoga with Seal playing in the background.

I found myself loving the yoga and Pilates parts, especially the stress-relieving locust pose, and the rewarding and mind-erasing corpse pose. But since yoga was just a small part of the video work out, my body was craving more. It became my mission to see what an actual yoga class might be like.

My spandex-infested gym in Boca Raton offered more than fifty classes each week, ranging from step to cardio slide. I noticed a flyer announcing a new class on the Saturday schedule: Power Yoga taught by an instructor named James, who brought his yoga knows from California. I showed up, not really sure what to wear, what to do, or even how to be. Dim lights, warm class, no shoes—and there was James, drop-dead gorgeous inside and out. His voice was spiritually mesmerizing, and his guidance from pose to pose was meticulous and magnetic.

And that started my yoga crush.

James expanded his class schedule and eventually opened one of the first power yoga studios in South Florida. As my agency grew, so did my stress level. Some of the girls from my office started going with me to the classes, and we soon had our own little tribe following James. He guided us mindfully with compassion, direction, and intention to places of physical and mental strength we never knew we had access to.

Yoga became part of the workweek, and as things got tougher, we would walk into a class frazzled from client meetings, campaign planning, and media pitching. I still did not realize the true power of yoga. I just knew my body was changing in very positive ways, and the results made me feel good inside and out. It was more of a physical thing. There was nothing I could do, or I had ever done workout-wise, that gave me the results of yoga. My body was lean, toned, and muscular.

Yoga inched its way into my life of what would become a committed relationship that is a never-ending practice of health, discipline that intersects both emotional and physical aspects.

How and Why Yoga Works

There is nothing perfect about yoga, including my practice. After experiencing an extremely difficult time in my life, I wanted to see if yoga could help bring me out of my riptide. The result? I created a hot yoga challenge for myself and made it a point to attend a yoga class every day for thirty days straight. The results were beyond my imagination, I came out of the thirty days balanced, recovered, and restored.

So, here's my list of 15+ reasons to incorporate yoga into your daily life as a means of physical and mental well-being:

Sweat. Losing what felt like gallons of sweat each week was like wringing out all the negative toxins, cleansed my insides, and resulted in some awesome mental clarity.

Sanity. Hormones, stress, lack of sleep, and life's everyday pressures can cause self-inflicted insanity. I felt my sanity meter move into the positive after my thirty-day yoga binge.

Perspective. This is a biggie. The difference in perspective from the time you enter a class and the time you come out is pretty significant.

Burn. Yoga poses might seem like you're just standing there, but the burn in your muscles gets the blood and circulation flowing.

Space. The space you give yourself in your day is the best present you can give your mind and body.

Surrender. At some point, there's a sense of surrender in yoga where you give yourself up to the "what is" and forget about "what is not."

Peace. Quieting the noise in your brain isn't easy, but giving your brain a chance to be quiet and know that you're in a place of safety, security, and positivity is essential.

Reset. We all know how to reset our computers. A yoga class is like a reset button; it optimizes your mind and body.

Satisfaction and accomplishment. I loved "checking in" to my yoga classes and tracking my progress.

Happiness. My mood dramatically shifted from depths of despair to happy emojis. There is a yoga pose called "happy baby," and you really get that feeling from the after-effects of yoga.

Positivity. As negative as things can seem in front of you, walking into a yoga class is almost like a tunnel. When the class is finished, you walk out a different door, and it opens your mind to a new perspective.

Hope. Impossible is not just a word; it is a feeling, so impossible is not a fact. Sometimes, it's hard to remember that feelings aren't facts. Nothing is impossible, and yoga replaces the feeling of impossible with the glimmer of hope we all need.

Acceptance and forgiveness. These are two biggies that I lumped into one because it seems you can't have one without the other. Being able to accept and forgive is not easy and does not come with a guarantee if you do one yoga class. The message here is that it helps get you there, to be one to accept and forgive or be on the flip side of asking for acceptance and forgiveness.

Creativity and ideas. In most yoga classes, there are a few minutes of meditation at the end, but throughout the class, it is difficult to let your mind wander. Your focus is for the most part of the class. This opens up special places in your brain that allow some of the best ideas and thoughts that you would otherwise probably not trigger. My ultimate problem-solving or creative ideas—whether it be a headline, interior design idea for my house, or a gift for someone—came during or after a class. Unofficial studies show the best ideas come as an after-effect of a yoga class.

Strength and flexibility. I'm talking physical, mental, and emotional here. A sixty-minute hot power yoga class can burn up to six hundred calories, and in just one week, you will notice a dramatic improvement in flexibility. You can count on yoga to give you increased muscle strength, improved respiration, energy and vitality, and improved metabolism. Factor in weight loss, cardio and circulatory health, improved athletic performance, and it will even protect you from injury.

You don't need a crisis or major life event to practice yoga. You don't even need Cindy Crawford or any celebrity instructor. All you need is a place to put your matt. This can be a yoga studio, hotel room, your bedroom, or your backyard.

#DigitalDetoxSecrets
Check out Glo as a yoga resource to help get you started from anywhere, any time, at any level.
Like anything, the hardest part is getting started.

The After-Party

If you're ever in Boca Raton, check out my first and favorite yoga studio Yoga South, where you will find James.
Other Florida fave studios include my Yoga Joint, Orlando Power Yoga, Guruv Yoga and AllI Island Yoga.

"Practice and all is coming!"
–K. Patabhi Jois

···4···

How CBD Oil Can Change Your Life

IMAGINE TRAVELING ALL day across three time zones, arriving at your event, and heading straight to a dinner party. You wake up early the next day for a public breakfast, and in less than two hours, you have to be ready to walk on stage as the keynote speaker. No big deal, said no one ever.

Did I mention this was 8,000 feet up in the mountains? Lack of sleep, new attitudes, and the stress of being the center of attention aren't a winning combination. Talk about serious imposter syndrome and the taste of vomit.

As I sat at breakfast contemplating a Bloody Mary or a Xanax, I saw this man peddling what looked like a magic potion in the form of a bottle and dropper. That seemed curiously illegal yet perked my interest as to what everyone was oohing and ahhing about.

Will Kleidon sat next to me with his elixir and introduced himself. Little did I know he was the founder and CEO of Ojai Energetics, leaders and innovators in the hemp-side of the health and wellness industry. Will pulled out a dropper and asked me if I'd like some CBD oil to take the edge off and help any altitude or hangover feelings I might have.

Wait, is this like liquid marijuana? No. Will explained the difference between CBD oil and THC.

CBD oil is all about getting healthy, not getting high.

Will put a dropper full of this earthy yet sweet liquid under my tongue. Okay, that was weird. Thirty seconds later, I started feeling significantly better.

The "I'm not good enough to be here" thoughts in my head started subsiding.

My brain started feeling less foggy and less anxious. Focus, calm, and purpose joined the conversation, and within 10–15 minutes, my physical and mental attitude was zapped with a new state of clear and present consciousness.

I snapped a picture of the bottle so I could remember to research what the hell had just happened.

Time was ticking for my presentation, so I packed it up and headed to my room to get ready. The next two hours flowed flawlessly like no other.

What is CBD oil?

To put it in simple terms, CBD is the part of the hemp plant that doesn't get you high, it just has tons of medical benefits. This is different than THC, which is what gives you that high feeling from marijuana. While some CBD oils can have very small trace amounts of THC, it's nowhere near enough to get you raiding your pantry or feeling anything at all.

If you like it a little more technical, according to Honest Marijuana, CBD stands for cannabidiol. It's one of a group of chemical compounds called cannabinoids. Tetrahydrocannabinol (THC) is perhaps the best-known cannabinoid, but others include cannabigerol (CBG), cannabicyclol (CBL), and cannabicitran (CBT), just to name a few.

Where in the world is Will?

I had to track down this guy Will who introduced me to the CBD oil secret sauce. This was a huge unlock. I caught up with him to find out exactly how and why he started Ojai Energetics and how I could get my hands on some more to spread the CBD oil love.

"I became interested in CBD around 2014. I'd studied the benefits of CBD but was looking for a CBD oil that was free of preservatives and certified organic, which wasn't on the market at that time. When I started to look into producing one myself, I met a chemist who taught me how we could make a formula that would be not only completely organic but also water-soluble, which would be a tremendous improvement on its bioavailability in comparison to other products," said Kleidon.

Benefits of CBD Oil

While CBD has been marketed for anxiety and conditions such as epilepsy, CBD oil has significant health and wellness benefits.

Sleep, pain, and anxiety. The top three problems modern humans have are poor sleep, general pain, anxiety. The correct application of CBD resolves all of these.

Depression, anxiety, and mood. CBD oil can reduce depression and anxiety and has been shown to provide an increase in your overall mood.

Heart and blood pressure. CBD oil has benefits for the heart and circulatory system, including the ability to lower high blood pressure.

Neurological disorders. Studies show that CBD is extremely effective at treating neurological disorders like epilepsy and multiple sclerosis.

Brain function. CBD is proven to increase brain cell production in multiple regions of the brain.

Work and school focus. CBD enhances response time, reflexes, etc. and is excellent for work.

Acne. CBD oil has lots of anti-inflammatory properties to reduce the appearance and occurrence of acne.

Will Kleidon's Digital Detox Secrets

Wake-up routine
I like to be around nature to ground myself. I wake up every morning, drink water first, ground myself, and set my intentions for the day.

Grounding and some
Walking barefoot because this makes a huge difference with all of the EMFs that we are exposed to. Also, lots of water and exercise and a good diet.

Personal wellness tip
Will's personal tips for a digital detox are to get outside, get around plants, and get away from fluorescent lights.

The After-Party
Catch up with Will Kleidon and Ojai Energetics if you want more CBD oil goodness. The company offers some of the most advanced water-soluble CBD oil products on the market.

Follow Ojai Energetics on Instagram and Facebook. @OjaiEnergetics

Get your first dose of Ojai Energetics using the code **buyer** for a digital detox secrets discount.

···5···

The Skinny on Skin

ARE THE DIGITAL devices we stare at each day putting our pores to the test? Our skin is not only our largest organ, but it is also the most susceptible to the dangers of digital overexposure. Televisions are only one hundred years old. The iPhone came on the scene in 2007, and now fast-forward to today, and it seems everybody has a smartphone glued to their hand.

I caught up Dr. Trevor Cates, known by fans as The Spa Doctor. She is the author of *Clean Skin from Within: The Spa Doctor's Two-Week Program to Glowing, Naturally Youthful Skin* (Fair Winds Press, 2017). A naturopathic physician, Dr. Cates was the first woman licensed as a naturopathic doctor in the state of California.

She was also my condo mate at my first Baby Bathwater event, a mastermind community for like-minded entrepreneurs.

Dr. Cates and I really got to know each other on the car ride back to the airport when she filled me in on her skincare practice and product line. We said our goodbyes, and she handed me a box of free samples, and I thought to myself, *just another schmoozy skincare line.* I'd already spent years sucked up in promising informercials, makeup counter sales pitches, and direct marketing miracles and "knew" nothing really lives up to its promises. And a four-step daily program? Not happening. I was lucky to get my makeup off some days.

Dr. Cates seemed to know her shit. In a practice spanning twenty years, she invested a ton of research on figuring out her skin and her patient's skin.

She explored the depths of the effects of how lifestyle and diet penetrate and impact our skin. She has developed skin-friendly dietary recommendations, best practices for a lifestyle that promotes healthy skin, and a line of natural skincare products designed for all skin types—all with a digital detox in mind.

"Our skin is an amazing opportunity for us to have an outer reflection of what's going on with our bodies internally," she says. "It gives us a lot of clues about our overall health, and there's so much we can do from the inside out to help our skin."

Digital Reflections on Skin

"Our digital habits can impact our skin, which acts as a sort of magic mirror that reflects back our stress," Dr. Cates notes.

Anything that impacts our adrenals, which help us manage stress through regulation of cortisol, can have an effect on our skin. When we experience stress, more cortisol is released, and this can have an inflammatory effect on our body. Existing skin issues such as eczema, psoriasis, or acne can worsen during periods of stress in our lives.

Indirectly, the light emitted from our digital devices can also wreak havoc with the skin. By interfering with our sleep patterns and moods, digital devices can create or exacerbate the stress that generates that cortisol-related inflammatory reaction. We need our dark time to help with melatonin production in order to get a good night's sleep, but did you know that melatonin offers skin benefits, too? Ideally, you want to produce your own melatonin, but taking a supplement can be beneficial when you just aren't getting enough natural sunlight.

Vitamin D, a hormone generated when our skin is exposed to the sun, is important for skin health and helps support a strong immune system, too. Vitamin D is made in the skin, and our bodies can store it in spring and summer for use later in the year when the sun is farther away.

Vitamin D is Key

To naturally increase your Vitamin D, make sure you're getting outdoors in better weather and exposing your arms and legs to sunlight for ten to fifteen minutes a few times a week. Make sure you are using a sunscreen with SPF protection from zinc oxide if you are spending time in the sun. If you suspect that you may be deficient in Vitamin D, Dr. Cates suggests that you get to a lab for a simple blood test. Ideally, she says, your level will be in the high range of normal. If you are on the low end of normal or below normal, take a Vitamin D supplement.

CBD for Skincare

CBD skincare products are raging in popularity right now, becoming the "it" ingredient in beauty products. But Will Kleidon of Ojai Energetics said choosing the right brands that have its products tested by an independent third-party lab is essential for your skin health and getting the most bang for your buck.

He recommended scanning the ingredients label for "full-spectrum CBD" or "full-spectrum hemp," "CBD oil" or "CBD extract." If you see only "cannabis sativa oil," "hemp seed oil," or "hemp seed extract," on the ingredients label, it has been made from only the seeds of the hemp plant, instead of the parts of the plant, that contain CBD. Hemp seeds contain little to no CBD.

"The cannabis plant produces over 418 compounds," Will said. "While CBD might be the trumpet section, what the body needs is the trumpet section playing with the whole orchestra."

#DigitalDetoxSecrets

What else can you do to combat the effects of a digital lifestyle to support healthier, nourished, clean skin?

Say no to an antibacterial solution on your hands (or on your phone, which then touches your face).

Yes, phones carry a lot of bacteria, and you want to avoid having that transfer to your facial skin by holding the phone against your head for calls. But Dr. Cates notes that we have a delicate ecosystem of organisms on the skin that protect it from bacteria. You do not want to upset that balance with harsh chemicals that kill off the good bacteria. Instead, wash your hands regularly and use headphones for calls.

Be proactive in nourishing your skin.

Eat foods that nourish your skin from the inside out. Be mindful what you put on your skin. There's a mild acidity that protects our skin, and we need to be careful not to upset that balance. Using soaps, cleansers, and other products with a high pH—or simply rinsing with water, which has a neutral pH—does not support that natural mild acidity. Look for products with antioxidants such as Vitamin C, Vitamin E, and CoQ10 to protect and support healthy skin.

Live a digital life supporting healthy skin.

What you do every day is the most important factor in skin health, Dr. Cates says. Your everyday choices make the biggest difference. In that spirit, she has chosen a relatively low-stress lifestyle in an active community in Utah and makes time for meditation each morning. Most workdays kick off with a healthy smoothie to start the day off with skin and body-nourishing breakfast. Move your body every day, and make sure you get at least some exercise, then make time for facials and another pampering on occasion.

When looking to offset the digital impact on our skin, start with making sure your skincare products are made with the best ingredients.

Best skincare ingredients to look for:

1. Arnica extract

2. Ubiquinone (CoQ10)

3. Cranberry, pomegranate and/or raspberry seed oil

4. Black, green or white tea

5. Pichia/resveratrol ferment extract

6. Turmeric root extract

7. Ginseng root extract

8. Pineapple fruit extract

9. Chlorella (green algae) extract

10. Essential oils (such as bergamot and ylang ylang)

11. Rosemary leaf extract

Worst skincare ingredients to avoid

1. Fragrance

2. Formaldehyde and formaldehyde releasers (quaternion-15, diazolidinyl urea, DMDM hydantoin, bronopol, or imidazolidinyl urea)

3. Mineral oil and petroleum (also called petrolatum, petroleum jelly, and paraffin oil)

4. Parabens (propyl, isopropyl, butyl, and isobutyl)

5. Ethanolamines (diethanolamine [DEA], monoethanol-amine [MEA], and triethanolamine [TEA])

6. Oxybenzone (benzophenone), octinoxate, and homosalate

7. Hydroquinone (or tocopheryl acetate) and other skin lighteners

8. Triclosan and triclocarban

9. Coal tar ingredients (including aminophenol, diamino-benzene, and phenylenediamine)

10. Butylated hydroxyanisole (BHA)

I searched the world over for skincare products worth the investment of money much less time. Never would I imagine I'd take the time to do a four-step skincare program each day until I started using The Spa Dr. products. Mention code "digitaldetoxsecrets" for your personalized discount.

#Digital Detox Secrets

If you're looking for another organic skincare line, a brand I also am in love with is Annmarie Skin Care.

Why? They handcraft skin care—using organic and wild-crafted ingredients—that promises beautiful, glowing skin. They use a 3-step, *Wild. Beautiful. Process.*

To start, they carefully select organic and wildcrafted ingredients to meet the highest standards of equality for your skin and body.

They then infuse selected herbs into aloe vera and into skin nutritive oils. These are used as a potent base for all the products.

Next, they add additional natural plant extracts, skin supporting nutrients, and aromatherapy to make the most active and effective natural products available.

Rumor has it Annmarie Skin Care is coming out with a CBD skin care line, sign up and follow them on social to be the first to know. @Annmarieskincare

The After-Party

Catch up with Dr. Cates if you want more. She offers organic skin care, free consults, and tips through her blog and podcast. Follow her on Instagram and Facebook. @Thespadr

• • • 6 • • •

The State of Health, Thanks to Digital

WONDER WHAT YOUR family doctor is not telling you? Fad diets, fancy gym memberships, no activity, anxiety, stress and depression, multiple screens in your face, rushing to eat, sitting all day, waking up and going to sleep with social media, apps and no naps, mood swings.

Sound familiar?

How have our digital habits and tendency to be "on" 24/7 impacted our overall health? I turned to Dr. Paul Savage, a highly respected, thirty-year physician, for his insight and guidance.

We first worked together in 2004 when Dr. Savage launched the first of its kind bioidentical hormone therapy practice in the United States. He was one of the pioneers in the integrative health industry with a focus on hormonal balance following in the footsteps by the likes of Suzanne Somers, one of the first mainstream advocates of bioidentical hormones and health.

Optimizing your hormones by having a healthier lifestyle is one of the secrets to anti-aging in a digital age.

"Your hormone balance actually reflects your lifestyle, good or bad," said Dr. Savage. "It's not your hormones that are the problem; it's your lifestyle impacting the production of your hormones. As we age, our hormones decline, which ultimately can lead to chronic disease and health problems."

Sleep, nutrition, and physical activity all have a positive impact on hormone production.

Dr. Savage held what is undoubtedly one of the most stressful positions imaginable for ten years as he managed the night shift at the largest trauma center in the country in Detroit, Michigan. His memories of that time will resonate with so many who struggle to find balance today.

"I was overstressed, undersleeping, drinking, not eating well, smoking cigarettes—like so many ER doctors do," he says. "By the age of 35, I was 284 pounds and had high cholesterol, heart disease, was pre-diabetic and had low thyroid and obesity. I had all sorts of depression going on."

Another relatable fact: Dr. Savage was accomplished and successful in his career, but it was taking an unacceptable toll on his health.

So, what changed? It was when his own doctor recommended a seventh medication that Dr. Savage truly committed to changing his lifestyle to improve his health. He has now spent the last twenty years building a knowledge base to share with other physicians and their patients through software, physical centers, and other resources on integrative medicine.

"In integrative medicine, we're taking the best of traditional medicine—which includes all of the medications that we need to use, but with the realization that we don't want to use them forever—and combining it with all of the other elements of good health," he explains. "This includes nutrition, exercise, stress management, sleep management, and detoxification."

The Rise of Digital Toxicity

Each of these practices is important in supporting good health, but we've gradually moved away from them as technology and the digital world have permeated our lives. Our environment is changing, and we are no longer able to recognize all of the things we need to do to stay healthy.

The proliferation of misinformation about health that is published online each year is a major challenge that can result in what he calls "health dead-ends." These are activities, diets, or other initiatives we undertake with the best of intentions, but because they are based on misinformation, can actually make our health worse.

Incorporating integrative medicine into your lifestyle is critical, and it must be guided by a qualified healthcare professional. Here are just a few of the key elements of an integrative health plan, according to Dr. Savage.

Hormones are essential to good health.

Anabolic and catabolic hormones are constantly at odds inside your body as the former work on building you up, and the latter on breaking you down. Both types of hormones are of equal importance; after all, you need old tissues torn down and disposed of to make room for new ones.

The imbalanced hormones are a natural function of aging. As we reach middle age, our anabolic hormone production—the ones that build us up—starts to taper off. Estrogen and testosterone are two examples of anabolic hormones. We've known about menopause for thousands of years, but it's only recently that we've begun to understand the relationship between hormones and the overall state of a person's health as they enter mid-life.

In addition to this natural aging process, there are environmental and behavioral factors causing dramatic changes in our hormones. For example, a forty-year-old man today has about half of the testosterone a forty-year-old man had forty years ago. Why is that happening?

Dr. Savage explains, "Every single healthy thing you do for yourself increases your anabolic hormones and decreases your catabolic hormones. Our "good" hormone levels are another casualty of these changes in our environment."

These digital environmental and behavioral factors include:

- We are working more
- We are sleeping less
- We are eating more, and more often
- We are eating less healthy foods
- Our natural environment is more toxic

Everyone needs hormone supplements at some point in their life, Dr. Savage says, because no one enters the last quarter of the average lifespan with healthy hormones. We are simply up against too much interference and the natural processes of aging. Starting hormone replacement early on can be key to maintaining healthy levels rather than trying to repair the damage later on. We also need to make lifestyle choices that promote the production of anabolic hormones.

Reduce your risk of digital toxicity from constant connectivity.

Constant connectivity has the potential to impact each of us negatively. However, we're living in this unique era where the full impact of our digital lifestyle is not yet understood.

"We have people in their forties who have been using technology constantly for ten years, but then we have teenagers in the same state," says Dr. Savage. "In our younger clients, we're seeing that the brain does not develop creativity nearly as much as in those who are immersed in their environment."

Interacting with people in real-time, developing emotional intelligence, and processing various types of information are just a few examples of the development youth lose when they are hyperconnected to digital devices. This stunted emotional growth is a contributing factor in the political turmoil we're seeing today, he says.

As for the older population, we are starting to see a decline in our ability to retain information. Responses come back fast online, but we retain less of the information we ingest. Even the social skills we've learned earlier in life are being lost as we stop reinforcing good behaviors and fall into bad digital habits.

This digital toxicity has a detrimental effect on each of us and on society as a whole.

Understand that nutrition is the medicine you give yourself all day long.

According to Dr. Savage, nutrition is responsible for 70% of our health—good or bad. The healthiest method of eating is what we know today as ketogenic, although it's been known as many different things over the years. Follow his best practices for optimal nutrition:

- Eat a lot of colored vegetables

- Eat a reasonable amount of protein

- Eat a lot of good saturated and unsaturated fats

- Practice intermittent fasting; eat less often and eat smaller amounts

Individual foods such as beef aren't problematic, he says—it's the way in which they are raised and reach the table. Choose foods that are as close to organic and farm-to-table as possible. Take the time to investigate the farming practices behind the foods you use to nourish your body.

It doesn't matter what the underlying health condition is; if you eat better, you will feel better and *get* better.

Busted health misconceptions that are harming your best efforts.

Do you know who came up with the recommendation that we eat five small meals a day? It was a campaign by food giant Kraft designed to get people to eat more snacks.

You've probably also heard that breakfast is the most important meal of the day, and it is—for children. This old adage has been disproven for adults who do not need to fuel the massive growth children are experiencing.

The state of your health is a deeply personal issue with countless variables driven by your genetics, lifestyle, nutrition, and more. A practitioner of integrative medicine examines the whole you and takes each of these factors into account, taking the guesswork out of the steps you must take to enjoy your greatest health possible.

Digital Detox Secrets from Dr. Paul Savage

Forget the alcohol, try CBD oil and THC. He's a big fan of CBD oil as an anti-inflammatory. CBD oil can help reduce anxiety, promote sleep, and help relieve certain pains caused by chronic diseases and sickness. It also helps reverse inflammation. He notes THC is also far safer than alcohol with less negative side effects. Nobody died of a THC overdose, but alcohol can kill you.

Plug into IV Therapy. This can be as simple as B12 for hangovers, Myers Cocktail for inflammation, or chelation to treat heavy metal toxicity. Nutrition in food has dropped considerably over the last four decades. The nutrients we get in food have been curtailed, resulting in issues such as chronic fatigue, Lyme syndrome, and other autoimmune deficiencies caused by complex reasons.

The After-Party

Looking for some sources to take the next steps in digital detox secrets? Find a doctor on Forum Health or dive deeper into a book such as Suzanne Somers' *Ageless: The Naked Truth to Bioidentical Hormone Therapy* featuring a chapter by Dr. Paul Savage.

Section 2

WORKSTYLE—BUSINESS AND PRODUCTIVITY

... 7 ...

Suicide, Depression, and CEOs

One in three entrepreneurs live with depression and 30% of all entrepreneurs experience depression coupled with the shocking back -to back suicides of celebrity entrepreneurs Kate Spade and Anthony Bourdaine illustrate the increased risk of suicide in our culture.

THE STRUGGLE IS REAL!

Just ask Cameron Herold. He's known around the world as the "CEO Whisperer" and is the mastermind behind hundreds of companies' exponential growth. I caught up with him at a few events, and he shared his first-hand experience on how CEOs and entrepreneurs suffer from depression, loneliness, stress, and sadness. As a matter of fact – most CEOs have the eleven traits of bipolar disease. Scary and true.

Some days, things will go really well, and on other days, things will suck. And the level of stress you're under will generally magnify those transient data points into incredible highs and unbelievable lows at whiplash speed and huge magnitude.

Sound like fun? Most entrepreneurs say yes to at least five of the following questions. Do you?

Are you filled with energy?

Does your mind get flooded with ideas?

Are you driven, restless, and unable to keep still?

Do you often work on little sleep?

Can you be euphoric?

Are you easily irritated by minor obstacles?

Can you burn out periodically?

Do you act out sexually?

Do you feel persecuted by those who do not accept your vision?

Many extremely successful entrepreneurs are even clinically diagnosed as manic-depressive or having bipolar disorder (nicknamed the "CEO disease").

I asked him how digital can be used as a solution and what a digital detox might look like for a CEO or business owner. We talked through actionable takeaways if you are a CEO and also how to help friends/clients who might be struggling behind the success game face.

The reality is everyone gets stressed out, and sometimes the people who seem the most in control are slowly losing it.

"The normal human being gets a paycheck every two weeks; the entrepreneur pulls money out of business when they can afford to pay themselves," Cameron points out.

Cameron knows a thing or two about dealing with stress and finding balance. He's the founder of the COO Alliance, a bestselling author of four business books, and has been coaching business leaders for more than twenty years.

During this time, Herold encountered his fair share of stressed out, overworked entrepreneurs.

"Most entrepreneurs don't take time off to decompress, and they just continue to work and work and work and always chase after the horizon," says Herold.

Sound familiar?

He's not just *seen* it, he's experienced burnout on a personal level.

"There was a time when I was working from 7:00 a.m. to 7:00 p.m., then heading out to dinner with coworkers. I'd head home at 11:00 p.m., then wake up and do it all again the next day," Herold recalls.

"I wasn't exercising, twelve-hour days were my norm, I was drinking too many martinis, and constantly feeling the pressure of trying to catch up," says Herold.

Since then, he's learned how to set boundaries and create space for activities outside of work.

"I'm looking to build a full balance. If I'm at a cocktail party, I know that I want to hear what someone does for work; I want to hear what they do for fun. I want to hear what their hobbies are and what their passions are and what they're into and what they're learning. If all you do is work, you're becoming a pretty dull person. That's why I disconnect; I want to be a more rounded, full person and bring more to the party," says Herold

Digital Detox Secrets to Decompress

We've looked any many ways of finding (and staying) balanced here's what works for Herold.

1. Take intentional breaks from your mobile device

Leave your cell phone, and don't carry it with you constantly. You don't need to have it with you at all times.

"Don't even bring your phone to the restaurant. Don't bring it on the golf course," says Herold.

2. Say "no" to business books on vacation

Let vacations be true vacations. Herold leaves business books at home and doesn't listen to work-related podcasts while traveling.

"Instead, listen to music. Enjoy the sights. Read for fun."

3. Set boundaries and allow yourself to disconnect

"Avoid being constantly connected. Be okay with disconnecting and rest assured nothing will blow up," says Herold. "The reality is nothing is truly that pressing. There are no planes in the air, no lives at stake."

No one should be expected to be on 24 hours a day.

"You have to decide what you want, and I personally don't want to be always on," says Herold.

Establish a morning routine and start the day mindfully

Easier said than done, maybe.

Waking up and immediately checking your email sets a stressful tone for the entire day. Instead, start the day mindfully or even mindlessly. Herold bases his own morning routine on Hal Elrod's Miracle Morning Routine.

1. Start with silence

Start with silence in the morning. Take a moment to simply lie in bed, consider the day ahead, and reflect on things you're grateful for.

2. State positive affirmations

Create one to three positive affirmations and say them aloud every morning. Using positive affirmations can boost your self-esteem, create a stronger sense of self-worth, and even boost your problem-solving abilities throughout the day. Some examples of positive affirmations might include statements like:

- I am talented, smart, and capable of running this company.
- I live with integrity.
- I practice compassion.
- I am strong.

3. Visualize key events in your day

Have an important call or meeting? Envision its success. Eliminate what-ifs and stop stories.

4. Work-out

Get your blood moving and flowing to the brain, even if it's only for seven minutes.

5. Read and allow your mind to open up

Herold recommends reading something, whether it's a business book or a novel, for fifteen minutes every morning.

6. Journal

Spend an additional five minutes writing. You can write freely, keep a diary, make a bullet journal, or a gratitude journal.

7. Take a cold shower

Herold likes to take a cold shower to boost alertness. Cold or not, hopping in the shower is a great way to start the day.

8. Have breakfast and vitamins

Herold not only has breakfast but a daily dose of supplements and vitamins.

9. Establish daily goals

Set three goals for each day. Herold uses the app Commit to Three to stay accountable. Using the app, you can share and track goals with an accountability partner or an entire group. It helps Herold stay on track and motivated.

Balance is for everyone, including the C-suite and hustle-harder entrepreneurs. You don't have to give up your life and sanity to chase your dreams. In fact, finding balance will help you show up clearer and more focused in your professional life—and you'll actually be able to pause and savor in your successes!

Cameron Herold's books. He calls them cheat sheets for entrepreneurs.

Vivid Vision. Talks about how to get the entrepreneurial vision out of the mind of the CEO and into the hands of employees, customers, and suppliers

Meetings Suck. How to unsuck and fix meetings. He wanted to fix the root problem.

The After-Party

Catch up with Cameron Herold if you want more. He offers one-on-one coaching, workshops, and leadership training.

Follow him on Instagram and Facebook. @Cameron_Herold_Cooalliance

$$\bullet\bullet\bullet 8 \bullet\bullet\bullet$$

How Mindful Business Owners Cope

AFTER 20 YEARS of entrepreneurship and practicing yoga, I decided to write this book and get my 200-hour yoga certification as part of the research. My 200-hour certification came via the vibes of Tymi Howard, a 500 ERYT International Yoga Teacher, holistic health coach, and entrepreneurial owner of Florida-based Guruv yoga studios. She's a global yoga goddess.

I had the opportunity to interview her recently about how she uses mindfulness to cope with the pressure of running an international brand.

When Tymi launched her first yoga studio twelve years ago, the marketing strategy consisted of three primary channels: print magazines, postcards, and snail-mail. As the industry evolved and everything began moving online, she initially resisted the trend.

Mindful on Social Media

"I felt social media was impersonal," she explained. But as her yoga and teacher training business grew and went global, Tymi began to realize the benefits of being socially active. Now, it's how she stays connected and communicates with her students all over the world.

As much as social media can help us find our tribe and be connected to like minds, Tymi notes you need to take care to keep it from taking up too much of your time. She schedules time each morning for social media marketing and get it out of the way so she can move on and doesn't feel owned by it.

That doesn't mean she stays off Facebook, Instagram, and Twitter for the rest of the day. On the contrary, Tymi believes it is important to be responsive to those with whom we are connected. While she is online throughout the day, she is quick to respond and engage on social. Yet, when it's time to disconnect, she has no trouble setting the phone aside or putting it away to fully focus on other areas of her life. When she and her husband are home together, every digital device gets shut down.

Learning how to "turn off" is challenging. This is where yoga can help, even if you are traveling and can't find a local studio. The digital realm can be a negative influence on our lives if we abuse it, but it can be a wonderful force for good, too. When she is traveling between yoga teaching engagements, Tymi will go online and find a yoga session or meditation class to join.

Modern Mindfulness Apps

The ability to practice mindfulness from anywhere was the driving inspiration behind the Buddhify app. Founder Rohan Gunatillake is also the author of *Modern Mindfulness*. He first began meditating while at university and soon afterward began work for a large technology company in London. As his interest in meditation grew, he realized that what he was being taught felt very separate from the fast-paced, digital, urban life he was living (and indeed loving).

Alongside his many hours of formal meditation, study, and long retreats, Rohan went on a mission to find ways to integrate traditional mindfulness with the realities of his day-to-day life.

"The core idea of Buddhify is that this is meditation for people who don't have time to meditate," Rohan said.

"The majority of the practices we share are contextual or situation-based. You may not have time to do a twenty-minute meditation at home, but if you're already walking to work, traveling, or going to the gym and have access to your phone and headphones, it's much easier to bring meditation to you.

Training the Brain

There are so many forces out in the world trying to grab our attention that it's more important than ever to ground yourself consciously. Meditation enables us to train our mind, and there are a variety of techniques to support different goals such as enhancing focus, fostering connections with others, spurring creativity, and more.

"Meditation allows us to develop awareness and attention to bring that sense of calm and balance. We are no longer entangled and bossed around by internal and external forces. You can then use that stability to help you achieve different outcomes," Rohan explains.

Becoming more mindful helps business owners combat the detrimental effects of the stressors and pressures inherent to running a company. How can you become more mindful in ways that support your health and lifestyle goals?

Evaluate which apps or social networks are taking up your time in ways that may not be positive. Taking a break with a digital detox is a good start, but you need to learn to control your usage while your device is on as well.

Be aware of how using your phone makes you feel. It's important that you are mindful while using technology, in addition to when you are taking breaks from it. Try to avoid using your device on autopilot and when you are bored.

Find new ways to use technology to support your well-being. Technology is here to stay, and it will become increasingly difficult to avoid it entirely. Use your device and connectivity as a tool to support good health, rather than in negative ways.

Keep an open connection between your body and mind with mindful breathing. Deliberately counter stress, fear, and other negative emotions you encounter while online by lengthening your body and focusing on deep, fulfilling breaths as you do in meditation or yoga.

Practice yoga to create new habits and neurological pathways. When you roll up your mat and step into the world after a yoga class, you are thinking and living differently. A regular yoga practice can positively influence your diet, relationships, career, and more.

Make yoga and meditation part of your daily routine. Tymi equates it to cleaning the cookies off your computer—if you don't remove the excess and clean up your headspace, you're going to get bogged down.

Use the power of mala beads and mantras, strands of 108 beads plus a "guru" bead traditionally used for meditation and prayer. Your beads are a constant reminder of the heartfelt intention or goal that you've set for yourself and can also help in your practice of repetitive mantras.

My fave source for mala beads is Bali Malas. Tymi is a brand ambassador for these fair trade, sustainable, eco-friendly products made with love and authenticity and stones in Bali.

Develop mantras that are meaningful and resonate. You might choose just a few short words, such as, "I am <u>strong</u>," or "I am peace." Or, you might find there's a Sanskrit mantra brings you to center. Find what works for you.

Learn to be an observer. Mindfulness can help you look at the challenges in your life from a different perspective. You are still present but can release the tension you feel around an issue in order to simply observe and meditate on it.

#Digital Detox Secrets

An easy way to get started in meditation using Buddhify. Download the app, and when you wake up in the morning, instead of hitting snooze for an extra fifteen minutes, go to the 'Waking Up" track and start your day with the seven-minute "Shine" meditation or the five-minute "Warmth" or both.

End your day with an easy mediation moment like by hopping under the covers fifteen minutes early and going to sleep listening to the thirteen-minute soothing meditation called "Fade."

My other Buddhify favorite guided meditations are

'Work Break/Ready" perfect for preparing to give a presentation or compete in an event. I use the 'Ready" meditation to get me grounded for a speaking gig or an important call.

Check out the book Malas, Mantras, and Meditations by Tymi Howard to crack the code of combining mala beads, daily mantras, and your meditation.

The After-Party

Check out the book Malas, Mantras, and Meditations by Tymi Howard to crack the code of combining mala beads, daily mantras, and your meditation.

Follow her on Instagram and Facebook. @TymiHoward

Looking for a new podcast, Rohan hosts Meditative Stories. Meditative Story is a first-of-its-kind podcast listening experience that combines the emotional pull of immersive storytelling with the immediate, science-backed benefits of mindfulness practice. Meditative Story is a WaitWhat original series — created by the team who built and led TED's media organization — in close partnership with Arianna Huffington's Thrive Global. The series is made possible with generous support from Salesforce

••• 9 •••

Avoiding Digital
Hoarding Disasters

BEHIND EVERY EMAIL is a person trying to get something done. They want you to *do something*.

Buy this.

Help that.

Write this.

Promote that.

Review this.

Fix that.

Every day last year, approximately 270 billion emails were sent and received. DMR reports show that this translates to an average of 121 emails received per day for the average office worker.

If you own your own business or side hustle, you might be contending with an even greater volume of email on a daily basis. Add to that a seemingly endless stream of social media notifications, text messages, news alerts, and other communications all vying for your attention, and it's a wonder we get anything done at all.

What's more, all of these business-related messages can take a real toll on our mental health. Higher levels of email activities cause more negative stress and lower chances of happiness.

Years ago, I made a New Year's resolution proving so impactful I've adopted it as a regular part of my routine: *to create more space in my life for opportunity.*

The first time I took this pledge, I was writing the first edition of *Social PR Secrets.* Making more space in my life meant strategic business planning in order to get myself off projects, transition staff to cover for me, and delegate or say no to new opportunities. Charlie Gilkey of Productive Flourishing, my coach, put me on a strict new writing schedule—every Monday, Wednesday, and Friday began with a yoga class from 9:00 to 10:30, after which I immediately went to the closest coffee shop with my laptop to write. No calls, no checking emails, and no social media sneaks. I wrote for two or three hours, then headed back to my office to answer emails and tie up loose ends for the day.

Resisting the urge to catch up on everything going on in my world right away was *hard.* What if I was missing out on *something?*

What if someone really, really needed me? Really?

I had to sort through these anxieties (some irrational, some completely legit) and force myself to stay the course. Before I knew it, my book was done!

It all seemed to flow, from down dog to up dog and out of my brain and through my typing fingertips.

Can you create more space in your life for opportunity?

Getting your digital hoarding tendency under control can help create the time, space, and focus you need to flourish.

Face it—social media takes up a lot of space in our lives.

If you work in marketing or PR in some capacity, the need for a digital detox (or alcohol) is almost inevitable. Whether it's for our personal or professional lives, social media is a space and time-sucker.

It's an endless task of reading, writing, posting, creating visuals, captioning, tagging, filtering, cropping, chatting, sharing, commenting, and don't forget the trusty old email inbox. With all of this to do, who has time for anything else?

We can't just buy more memory or storage, and our brains don't come with an upgrade option. Until this happens - here are a few tools and tactics you can use to reduce digital and social media clutter to free time, space, and energy in your life.

Prioritize and declutter your inbox with Unroll.me.
Finding a way to take control of the more than 2,300 email subscriptions I had accumulated over the years was life-changing. Unroll.me is an email detox system that will get you unhooked from the email leaches you have signed up for in the past. It gives you the power to unsubscribe to any email subscriptions and "roll up" select emails into one easy-to-read magazine-like email, which includes all of the emails you want and need to review.

Upgrade your computer memory to make review faster.
On any given workday, I have more than twenty tabs open in multiple windows in three browsers. I also call and video conference with Skype and use Google Hangouts for chat and calls. Adding memory to my computer has already helped speed things up. Upgrade your computer to speed things up and save time. Unless you're technologically savvy, you may want to save yourself the time and frustration of doing this yourself and hire a professional. It may not save you hours a day, but ultimately, this will reduce the time you spend on each task and cumulatively as a result.

Clear your cookies with meditation.
Some years back, I came across an article in *Marie Claire* about how women are using mediation as a business strategy and how it gives them an upper hand in negotiating and communicating to get what they want. Interesting, right? Into looking into it further, I found an article in *Psychology Today* on how meditation also influences weight control, reduces anxiety, increases empathy and compassion, and improves memory function.

Meditation can help us all to be more rational, creative, and likable people. I'm sold! You don't need to interrupt your workday to make a difference with meditation, either. Get an app like Buddhify and take brief meditation breaks throughout the day. This allows you to "clear your cookies" before moving on to the next task so you can approach it with fresh eyes and renewed energy.

Employ Zappos CEO's Yesterbox technique for tackling a large volume of email.
Tony Hsieh, CEO of Zappos, recommends using an email management method called Yesterbox in which you separate your inbox into six different folders:

- **Yesterbox.** Emails you received yesterday. Depending on your email account, there are multiple ways to ensure that your mail from yesterday ends up in this folder without having to manually move each one individually.

- **Today.** Strictly for same-day emails; it's important to keep it separate from the Yesterbox mail.

- **Action Required.** All emails that require task completion or follow-up.

- **Awaiting Response.** Important emails from upper management or clients who need responses as soon as possible.

- **Delegated.** Emails you've forwarded to other employees or team players.

- **Archive.** Emails you want out of your inbox but aren't ready to delete; a temporary trash can.

Using this system, you can simultaneously manage your inbox while creating a to-do list for yourself based on yesterday's mail. Schedule time in the morning to sift through and organize your Yesterbox.

Reduce notification volume.
Do an audit of all social network notification settings and turn off the ones you don't need. You can eliminate the email notifications from social media entirely. Do you need to be notified every time someone likes your update? Really? Or do you need a daily digest from a LinkedIn group? Maybe a weekly or monthly digest is sufficient. Consider your needs and let everything else go.

Audit your time spent in email and schedule it into your day accordingly.
Check out RescueTime, a service that helps you figure out where you spend your time and if you might be spending too much time on email. The average person spends four hours a day on email alone. Even if you could shave off one hour a day, that would give you back five hours a week to do something more productive and enjoyable, like a yoga class or writing a blog post. Using services like Mailstorm, Boomerang, or Sanebox can make sure you never miss an important email from a source or a story lead but still have space to focus on writing.

Quit wasting time with unnecessary follow-up emails and phone calls.
Streak or HubSpot shows you who has opened your pitch email. Coming from the public relations world, we know journalists hate when you call and say,
"I was just following up to see if you received my email."

55

I am an admitted B-I-T-C-H to an unsolicited sales-like call.

Make sure you track the time you are saving and the space you are creating in your mind and routine for more opportunity. You'll be amazed at what a little proactive, intentional time management can achieve.

The After-Party

To find all the resources, links, and more, check out DigitalDetoxSecrets.com

• • •10• • •

Empowering Business Events

YOU'RE UP WAY too early to get to the conference center, and after navigating traffic and transit in a strange city, get to the venue just in time to grab a carb-fused – pure sugar pastry and a coffee for breakfast.

You race to the first session and furiously take notes to take back to your team. Before it's over, you're already planning how you're going to put out a fire back at the office based on the emails you're getting from your clients and team. There goes your break time. Oh well, maybe you can relax for a few minutes at lunch? No such luck—there's that presentation you have to get sent off by this evening.

The typical marketing conference is a relentless frenzy of too much information, punishing seating, terrible Wi-Fi, overzealous scheduling, trying to juggle client work, and every kind of visual and auditory stimulus imaginable.

Pay attention over here! Get to that meet-up over there! Drink all the booze! Eat all the food! Make the superficial connections! Gather the leads!

Conferences are *exhausting. Stupid exhausting thanks to our over-ambitious and try to do everything mentality.*

Try these five digital detox secrets to reduce conference burnout and have a healthier experience:

1. Schedule buffer days.
Set up your out-of-office email responder to start one day before leaving and keep it on one day after you return. This gives you some breathing space before and after to get ready to leave and catch without feeling like you must respond to email in real-time.

Use your "out of office" message as an opportunity to educate and communicate a personalized message. You can even share a little about the conference you're attending and invite people to follow your conference adventure on Instagram.

2. Hydrate.
Travel is a surefire way to instantly dehydrate the body, especially if you're flying. Dehydration negatively impacts your focus, memory, mood, energy, sleep, and even your physical appearance. Mix in the abundance of alcohol served at conferences, and it can take days to recover.

Hydrate your mind and body by drinking at least twelve ounces of water every waking hour. If you really want to monitor your body's analytics, Thermos makes a water bottle that connects via Bluetooth to a FitBit to help you achieve your daily hydration goals.

3. Take "Me" breaks

It's easy to let the conference run your schedule, but planning ahead can put you in charge of creating space for yourself. Most conference schedules start in the early morning with sessions, events, networking happy hours, and dinners ending late in the evening.

Review the schedule ahead of time and find pockets of time you can reserve for yourself to take a mental *time-out* from crowds, emails, and unplanned events.

This could mean sleeping in, taking a nap or walk at lunch, or finding a quiet place to listen to a fifteen-minute guided meditation on an app like Buddhify.

4. Sleep more and drink less

There's an old saying "nothing good happens after midnight." If you don't get the chance to go out much, it's easy to get carried away in party mode when you see and meet industry friends.

In fact, a recent study reported that 27% of business travelers admit to binge drinking while at a conference or business trip. Do you really want to wake up the next morning looking at pictures of yourself on Facebook doing shots? Trust me. The answer is a big NO.

Give yourself a curfew and be the one to head in early. Getting a solid eight hours of sleep assures you will be fresh to take on the next conference day. It can also mean less alcohol intake and decrease the chances of being *over-served*, dehydrated, and hungover.

Need a reminder? Add an alarm on your phone to give you the nudge it's time to unwind and get ready to sleep.

5. Activate your full conference potential

Business conferences are starting to be more mindful of attendees' health and wellness.

For the first time, conferences such as Social Media Marketing World are factoring in a health and wellness agenda offering free yoga and movement classes to give attendees alternatives to networking.

Pubcon also added a session titled Social Media Health focusing on tips and advice for productivity and health while using social media for business.

Pack your sneakers, yoga mat, or favorite workout gear and carve out time to activate the mind and body.

Level up with digital detox focused events.

While getting offline to regroup and recharge is important, there's a special energy and camaraderie in doing so with like minds.

Now, there's an entire subset of conferences designed to help you do just that.

You've heard the old adage you should spend more time around those you hope to be like—this is the power in digital detox conferences and events.

I had the privilege of interviewing the creator of one such conference recently. Michael Lovitch, co-founder of the Baby Bathwater conference, decided to create an event to counter everything he hated about conferences.

Finding your mentors is critical

"The only way to really grow is to find the people who can help you. However, typical mastermind groups and conferences inherently attracted people who were trying to make a buck in whatever way they could, even if that meant spamming, scamming, or otherwise being a bad actor. In these groups," Michael said, "trust is important, and participants are reluctant to share their knowledge, insights, and vulnerability.

The best groups are curated, not with success metrics like revenue in mind, he says, but with an eye to personality and intention. The Baby Bathwater experience is a no-pitch environment offering an exchange of real value where participants are urged to be fully present. Its organizers have turned the traditional conference concept on its head by adding elements of a party, a retreat, and a mastermind. Those interested in attending must apply, and at the top of the application page, organizers state:

We don't care…

- How much money you make
- If you are considered "a big deal"
- Who you know

Instead, they want to see participants who fit the following description:

- You're a nice person—we're from small towns, and we're pretty good at reading people
- You're a "giver," not a "taker"
- You have useful business skills… You know what you're doing
- You LOVE who you're selling to… We call it the "Give a Shit" factor
- You aren't scamming people or doing anything unethical
- You're fun, easy to talk to, and self-reliant

You can learn more about this unique event at babybathwater.com.

For example, an event called Unplugged Fiji is another worldly opportunity to get off the grid and reset your priorities in the company of like minds. The focus here is strictly on relationship building and on connecting through shared experiences.

Open to just twenty fully vetted participants, it takes place over five days on the stunning tropical island of Fiji. According to organizers, "small groups allow us to drive relationships deep, and high curation allows us to learn and grow from amazing people so we can be ourselves and unplug in our own ways without judgment."

There must be something in the waters surrounding Fiji, as it's home to Cat Howell's epic, three-day Agency Accelerator, as well. This intensive training for freelancers and agency owners certainly has a business focus but also coaches participants in shifting their mindset for success. The fun part is it's not just Fiji, it can be Mexico or some magical place off the grid to unite and reset.

Do you invest as much in building relationships as you do in building revenue?

Whether you're taking in a traditional conference or planning a deep dive into a digital detox event, the perspective from which you view this opportunity is critical. Plan what it is you want to achieve rather than where you plan to be every moment of the day. Take care of yourself. Prioritize the connections you'll make.

Get off the *same old*, tried and true hamster wheel of events and break free on a new path.

Steve Chou, owner of My Wife Quit Her Job, teaches people how to start and grow a successful online business. He hosts events each year with the intent to foster deep relationships with other attendees.

Here is his tried and true formula using the powers of digital to manifest online and offline relationships quite similar to successful mastermind formulas of Baby Bathwater.

- **Sessions in close proximity.** By holding all the sessions in the same area, people were encouraged to mingle between presentations.

- **Everyone dines together.** Lunch was catered every single day so people were inclined to eat with each other. In addition, we had sign-up sheets for dinner to encourage group dining for attendees.

- **Open bar every night.** A little alcohol always encourages people to loosen up

- **Private Facebook group.** A record number of attendees created Facebook live video introductions leading up to the event. In addition, the speakers made videos as well, which made the FB group much livelier!

Make the time and space in your life to be truly present at the conference and to reap every possible benefit from the experience.

The After-Party

Learn more about Baby Bathwater @Babybathwater and Cat Howell @cathowell on Instagram. To find all the resources, links, and more, check out DigitalDetoxSecrets.com

• • • 11 • • •

Write Way to Power Through Procrastination

THERE'S NOTHING WORSE than sitting down at your laptop to stare at a blank page. Whether it's a blog post, press release, email, or entire manuscript you're trying to write, it's always easier to put it off for just another day.

Writing doesn't have to feel like a chore, like just another thing that takes up time you'd rather spend doing—well, just about anything else.

Secret Code: P-R-O-C-E-S-S

I get advice from writing coach and marketer Miranda Miller. She is the queen of helping professionals of all kinds improve, not only their writing quality and value but their process as well. She advocates for a systematic approach to writing that breaks each piece into accomplishable tasks. At each phase, there are tools and tips to help you move your writing forward.

"That blank page is daunting," Miranda shared with me. "You need to set yourself up to make small gains and give yourself more wins in the writing process, to stay motivated and truly enjoy the process of writing."

When her writers employ this strategy, she says, they dramatically reduce the amount of time they spend writing. On top of that productivity boost, they're able to get more creative and engaged. Actually, putting pen to paper (or fingers to keyboards) and writing is just one small part of the process—and it's much easier when you invest the time in preparing to write.

#Digital Detox Secrets

These are my fave four procrastination-busting steps to writing any type of content

1. Create your outline

This is a step that too many skip over, but missing it often results in frustration. You know you want to write about a specific topic. However, very rarely do the right words just fall out of your brain and onto the page in just the right order.

Go back to the basics and write the core elements your piece needs to have. For a blog post, the bare bones of your piece might look something like:

Title
Purpose (a single sentence that summarizes what the piece
    should accomplish)
Introduction
Body
Conclusion

Now, start dropping information you already have into each section. Maybe you have a statistic you want to include—does it belong in the introduction or is a better fit in the body of your blog post? Is there a next step you want readers to take? Pop that into your conclusion section. Use a bulleted list for each section. You aren't actually writing anything yet, only getting your thoughts and information organized.

2. Get serious about research

Now that you have some content in your outline, it's easier to identify gaps and areas you really need to build out. What's more, it's just good practice to make sure you fully understand what's new in the space you're writing in as this may shape your own views ahead of publishing your piece.

Miranda recommends that you incorporate these tools into your online research in addition to perusing social media and doing regular Google searches:

BuzzSumo allows you to search for the most read and shared content on any topic in the last year. You get three free searches per day with the free version. Agencies, brands, and other heavy users might choose to invest in the premium version, which allows for unlimited daily searches and also lets you filter results down to a more recent, shorter date range.

Answer The Public shows you what questions real people are asking about any given topic. It's a great way to learn more about the motivations and intent behind searcher's queries for information. Using a tool like this enables you to write from a more user-focused perspective; you're not only writing what you want to say but what people actually want to hear.

Google Trends brings back interesting audience insights that can help shape your writing. Does the level of interest in this topic change throughout the year? Where do the people who search for information about this live? What topics are related to this, and how many people are searching for those?

In exploring these insights, you'll discover alternative points of view, complementary content you may want to link your readers to, gaps in your own understanding of the topic, and more.

3. Gamify and socialize your writing

Writing doesn't have to be a lonely or solitary endeavor. Miranda hosts online writing groups in which participants do writing "sprints" based on Francesco Cirillo's Pomodoro Technique of time management.

In these sessions, writers break two hours of writing up into four Pomodoros or sprints of twenty minutes each. The goal for each Pomodoro is recorded in a shared tracking spreadsheet, which each writer updates after each writing sprint. At the beginning of the session, each writer briefly shares what they are working on and what their goal is for the next sprint. They have the opportunity to ask for input from the other writers if they are in need of an opinion or feedback.

Once the timer begins, each writer mutes their microphone and may choose to turn off their video. They are on their own to build out their piece for the next twenty minutes.

"Going into a writing sprint with an outline that is fleshed out, well defined, and adequately researched is a huge confidence booster," Miranda says. "What's more, your brain has had time to mull over the possibilities of the piece. Your story has been percolating while you've been doing other work, spending time with family, and even sleeping. By the time you sit down to write, your brain is already ahead of you and ready to go."

It's important that you give yourself permission to write freely and to resist the urge to edit as you go. This step is about getting your thoughts organized on paper, in sentence and paragraph structure.

Sometimes, she notes, people realize they need to do more research, and that's 100% acceptable. A writer might choose to dedicate an entire Pomodoro to finding more information to enrich the story.

Between Pomodoros, writers check off the portion they've completed and get that small win that drives the motivation to continue. They have a chance to chat and network with the other writers. Then it's back at it, alternating writing sprints and social breaks until the end of the session.

It's a technique you can incorporate into your solo routine, as well. Simply extend each Pomodoro to 25 minutes and reduce your break to 5 minutes between. Use your breaks to get up from the desk, shake out any stiffness, grab a glass of water, and disengage from the writing process (even if only briefly). You might even do a few quick yoga poses or take three minutes to meditate and clear out the cobwebs. At the end of your solo session, you'll have achieved one hundred minutes of writing in two hours.

4. Declutter and refine your writing with a three-step editing process

Breaking the editing process into three steps allows you to focus on specific objectives in each pass:

Substantive edit. In this pass, you focus on the overall flow, substance, and tone of your writing. If you need to cut entire paragraphs, change from first-person to third-person, adjust from casual to a more formal style, or otherwise make substantial changes to the piece, you'll do it here. If there are any sentences or words that do not further the readers' understanding of that point, they are superfluous and need to go.

Copy edit. In your copy edit, you'll focus on decluttering and refining the language used. This is where you'll eliminate redundancies, remove filler words like "that" and "very," repair run-on sentences, trim away jargon or slang/idioms, and otherwise polish your writing. Try a tool like Hemingway App to get instant suggestions on voice, style, grammar, readability, and more to improve your writing.

Proofread. This is your final review for spelling and grammar errors, formatting, typos, and other mechanical issues that need to be resolved before publishing. Grammarly's Chrome extension or desktop app for macOS is a must-have for online proofing. You may also want to print the piece and read it on paper to catch those tiny errors your eyes are likely to gloss over.

Approaching your writing in this way may seem arduous at first, but each small step that you take makes the next step easier. It can make the process more fun, healthier, and more productive, to boot.

The Law of Digital Attraction with Music

Power up your brain with the app Brain.FM It's a science-first approach creating music that sounds different–and affects your brain differently–than any other music.

Finding Your Flow

Just ask the flow expert, Steven Kotler. He is a New York Times bestselling author and an award-winning journalist and executive director of the Flow Research Collective. He finds his writing flow between the hours of 4:00 a.m. and 8:00 a.m. when distractions are low, and flow is at an all-time high.

> *"Flow describes these moments of total absorption when we become so focused on the task at hand that everything else falls away. Action and awareness merge. Time flies. Self vanishes. All aspects of performance—mental and physical—go through the roof."*
> *Steven Kotler*

The After-Party

Catch up with Miranda Miller if you want more. She offers exclusive writing education, coaching, networking, and content auditing.

Follow her on Instagram and Facebook. @Mirandamwrites

Section 3

SOCIALSTYLE— SOCIAL MEDIA, SELFIES, AND MORE

···12···

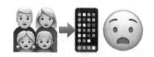

A Parent's Guide to Teens, Social Media, and Smartphone Addiction

WHAT HAPPENS WHEN you take a teen's phone away for seven days? Withdrawal symptoms similar to a drug addict. Panic attacks, anxiety, anger, crying, tantrums, screaming, rolling eyes, pissed-off body language, lies, pouts, disbelief. Parents of teens have it rough these days thanks to a new cocktail: smartphones laced with social media apps. The mix is so potent it can take over your teen's life and so dangerous it can literally open the door to stalkers.

Zombie Teens. The New Normal?

There is a teen epidemic happening right in front of us, and it's called smartphone addiction. If you are wondering why your teenager is always taking selfies, it's called Snapchat—better named Crackchat. Or Instagram and TikTok. Why?

Top ten reasons my daughter "could not live" without her phone (in her words)

1. Friends would be mad

2. Losing her streaks (more on this below)

3. FOMO (fear of missing out)

4. That's where she hangs out with friends

5. Netflix

6. "Not fair"

7. No other way to talk to friends

8. YouTube

9. She'd rather lose her voice calling phone app than Snapchat

10. Boredom

Teen brain hacking

Apps like Snapchat are actually designed to be addicting. It's called brain hacking, and developers are hired to study the brain and the neurological triggers that keep us coming back for more. According to a former Google product manager, Silicon Valley is engineering your phone, apps, and social media to get you hooked. It's all about the Likes.

The problem for parents today is that the apps sprout up so fast that it's hard to keep up with new ones as quickly as they are available for download. Most apps do not come with any age limits, warning labels, or ratings that parents can easily screen.

Dear Parents: Have you checked the children?

If you have a teenager, you might need to do a checkup. There is a social media crisis happening right in front of your screens.

My daughter just turned fifteen, and I've watched the social media highs and lows influencing her circle of friends the past few years. As a social media expert for businesses and the instructor of the social media management class at the University of Florida, I thought I was more social media savvy than most parents. In my mind, I could easily maneuver my teenager through the dangerous minefields of social media. Little did I know I was in parenting La La Land.

At age twelve, she wanted to join Snapchat, and I resisted for about a year. Finally giving in when she was thirteen with the understanding it would only be used with her friends, we joined. Snapchat, once coined for teen sexting in 2012, is now one of the most popular social media networks with all ages hooked, even Wall Street. I added Snapchat to my Social PR Secrets book and my college class curriculum and thought this would also allow me access to keeping up with my teen's snaps and stories.

My first wakeup call.

I realized I actually knew nothing about teens and social media until last year when I read American Girls: Social Media and the Secret Lives of Teenagers by Nancy Jo Sales. The book is an alarming and eye-opening study of more than two hundred teenage girls and their social media and Internet habits and behavior. American Girls is a must-read for all parents of teens and preteen girls purely as a way to take a deep dive real look at what's happening on the inside of our girl's lives. Trust me, this is a side you will not be exposed to as a parent no matter how much you know about social media. Think nude selfies, slut-shaming, and viral cyberbullying.

Snapchat Takeovers

In my world, a Snapchat takeover is a good thing for brands; it's how businesses can reach younger audiences and influence the market. In our teen's world, Snapchat is taking over their lives and hacking their brains.

Thanks to Snapchat, Instagram, TikTok and other apps like Houseparty, teens don't think they need to hang out in person anymore. They don't talk on the phone, either. Everything happens in private and in disappearing messages or live videos. Even when friends are together in the same room or sitting in the backseat riding home from school, there's a mobile device stillness in the air. It's Snapchat silence, scrolling, staring, and selfies.

Minimal conversation except a few, "Did you see that?" "OMG, can you believe she is with him?"

As a parent, it became very annoying every time I was in the car with my daughter, riding in silence because all she was doing was watching the drama unfold on Snapchat like it was a TV show and taking pictures of herself every ten seconds to keep up with her Snapchat streaks.

And what's a streak you might ask?

A Buzzfeed article put it perfectly: a Snapchat streak is the number of days in a row that you and another person have mutually sent and opened at least one Snapchat. While they are "fun" and all, Snapchat streaks can strain any friendship or relationship.

Buzzfeed reported that Snapchstreak anniversaries are more important than birthdays. If your teen currently has one (or thirty) going, you should be aware that streaks can suck time and energy from more important things in life.

The struggle is real for all teenagers today.

The pressure is always on for teens. They expect an immediate response from each other, whether it is a text or message on

Snapchat. They pay close attention to who is doing what with who and where. Teenage girls can be notorious for drama and adding social media to the mix takes it to all-new levels that can lead to death-defying circumstances. Just look at the rise of teenage suicide well marked with the latest controversial Netflix series *13 Reasons Why*. The series studies the impact of how teens treat each other and how small aggressions can have unthinkable effects even without the power of social media.

What made me pull the plug?

My breaking point happened when my teenager and one of her good friends had a falling out on Snapchat. It was not just between the two of them; it was in real-time unfolding in snaps, stories, and live videos. Other friends were involved, taking sides and making comments.

We are so used to unfollowing and unfriending in a click of a button that our teens are being programmed to think real life unfriending is the new normal, that it's okay just to block a friend one day and unblock the next day. Instead of learning compromise, conversation, and conflict skills, teens are learning it's easier just to ignore your problems, i.e., block.

We have no idea what's happening in someone's life on the other end of the screen. The problem with social media is it robs our teens of empathy and compassion they would more likely have in a face-to-face communication versus hiding behind the taps and scrolls of the smartphone.

I've always monitored my daughter's digital use with apps such as AT&T Smart Limits and Life360 more from a safety perspective. In ninth grade, I realized that her app and phone interaction was happening during school, after school, homework time, and dinner time, and there seemed to be no beginning and no end. It was getting out of control, so I found an app to monitor screen time and block her apps during school, bed, and study times. This worked somewhat, and I promised her that, come summertime, I would take off the restrictions to give her more free time for her friends on social media. Big mistake.

No phone, no apps for seven days

It devastated me to see my daughter and her friends dealing with so many unnecessary distractions and interactions. With summer just beginning, things were not off to a positive start. I could see she needed a break. Her Snapchat feed was robbing her of more important and memorable things. I asked what she saw the value was in Snapchat? Was it replacing summer reading, family awareness, responsibilities, goals, mindfulness, physical activity, mental stimulation, and even her natural sweetness? Yes was not a possibility. I was done. Not everything had to be for the selfie or the photo opp.

So, I took her phone away entirely, the most crippling thing a teen could ever imagine. There was no time frame. Even I did not know how long I could do it since this would also be hard for me not being able to get in touch with her when I was not with her.

It was not easy, but the benefits were amazing, and I could never have expected better results.

Day 1. Denial and isolation. I deleted the social media apps from her phone, and she found a way to get on them from another device.

Day 2. Lots of anger. I figure out she's going behind my back and using her apps from her friend's device. She changes her account passwords and gives them to another friend to manage her social media and keep up her daily Snapchat streak. Her phone is taken away completely, and I change all her passwords. Withdrawal symptoms are at an all-time peak, and bargaining starts to happen.

Day 3, 4, and 5. Luckily for both of us, she is volunteering full-time at an art camp for community hours.

Day 6. Spiritual awakening begins as my fifteen-year-old realizes that being clear and present is not so bad. I take her away for a night at our condo on the beach as a means to disconnect from the last few days and connect with each other. We take our usual walk on the beach, and she starts asking me what my grandmother was like. We end up walking for three miles with me telling all of my memories of growing up with my grandma in Chicago.

Day 7. We watched movies, hung out together, and went to the beach. That night, she handed me a three-page letter telling me what a great weekend she had with me and loved hearing all the stories.

Danger signs

- Streaks with more than five friends
- House party app
- Stalking and spying on where other friends are
- Fake social media accounts with multiple identities
- Closed and secret Facebook groups
- Apps that hide images such as Vaulty
- Cleared search history on phone browsers
- Tracking location settings and features
- Relationships with friends they have never met
- Unfriending in real life

Did you know that teens can also block certain people from seeing their Snapchat stories, such as their parents?

Shocking Stat

Common Sense Media found that 30% of teens who are online believe their parents know "a little" or "nothing" about what social media apps and sites they use.

Signs your teen is addicted:

- Not answering your text messages

- Not answering phone calls

- Up all night and/or in bed all day on their phone

- Not responding in conversation

- Forgetting

- Blank stare

- Stressed face

- Not telling the truth

- Secretive behavior

- Turning on and off location settings

- Freak out if their phone is not with them at all times

Make sure you have your teen's:

- Apple ID and password

- Phone passcode

- Email passcodes

- Computer passcode

Restrictions and allowances

Is social media a right or a privilege? Smartphones used to be a luxury, but today, most parents see them as a communications and safety necessity. But you would not let your teens grab a red solo cup and stay out all night, would you? Then why let them congregate on social media anytime they want? There is no real need to get together in person with friends. Grounding your teen from participating is not any threat anymore since they will just meet up with their friends anyway on Snapchat or Houseparty.

Digital Detox Secrets

- OurPact. This app allows parents to control the screen time of certain apps and shut down apps during certain hours, such as bedtime, school, and study time.

- Life360. Allows you to track the location of your teen and all family members who join. It reduces stress and needs to check in with each other.

Gaming the Social Media System with Teens

Advice from entrepreneur and mom Shelly Kramer

My favorite part of each day in the summer is quickly becoming watching my kids work through the "to do" lists that I made and taped to the fridge for each of them.

- Bed making

- Teeth brushing (amazing it has to be on a list to happen)

- Breakfast making

- Cleaning up a room

- Doing something creative for twenty minutes

- Being outside for twenty minutes
- Exercising for twenty minutes
- Reading for twenty minutes
- Writing for twenty minutes
- Doing something to help someone

It's infinitely easier to let them be the masters of their days, which usually means they watch videos or dive into electronics all day so they don't bug me. But they really enjoy the fact that they know they're expected to get through everything on the list before they can do that, and they take it seriously. This was not my idea. However, I owe a big thank you to whomever it was I stole it from. It works!

Parents, you have choices.

1. Do nothing and take your chances.

2. Do something and give your teens boundaries they can't give themselves and ones you have never had to experience.

Even our college-aged kids agree. They say teenagers today have it so much harder with pressure and stress than they ever imagined just a few years ago.

For Immediate Release
Snapchat streaks and Instagram hearts are not college requirements.

Like alcohol and drug addiction, teens need parents to guide and support them in balancing the necessary evils of smart-phones and social media. It's an evolving work in progress and not something we can set up and forget.

···13···

Why Your Teen Won't Get Into College

IF YOU VISUALIZE the day your child gets accepted into college, think again. I want to share some news with parents: social media mishaps are one way to significantly increase the chances of getting denied from that first-choice university or even kicked out.

Yes, my golden child might have a perfect GPA, all the right requirements, and be a model student in real life, but what's been happening behind the scenes of social media can ruin everything.

And guess what, there's no such thing as Snapchat University.

Colleges and universities are beginning to have zero tolerance for inappropriate social media behavior. Harvard University rescinded admissions offers to at least ten students who shared offensive images within what they thought was a private Facebook group chat. Getting into college is more than just essays and SAT scores. Social media footprints can make it or break it when it comes to passing the admissions officer seal of approval.

In a Kaplan Test Prep survey of more than 350 college admissions officers in the U.S., 35% polled reported having looked at applicants' social media accounts to learn more about them.

Privacy, both personal and disappearing, is almost not possible in today's world. Private groups are technically private, but anything shared, even in a text, can be screenshot and then publicly shared in a way that can spiral out of control and go viral.

But wait, Snapchat content "disappears" so what can go wrong? Everything and anything. It starts with simple as a screenshot that gets saved and possibly published on a public social media account.

Profanity and "questionable" language

Sexually explicit content—memes and messages

Nudes—in case you did not know, teenage boys routinely text girls they know for nude pictures of themselves, called "nudz."

Politically incorrect content

Negative or offensive content targeting a minority group

Brandishing of weapons

Alcohol and drug-related content

Which social media platforms matter for college admissions? All are fair game because even the most obscure social media network, digital image, or communication can get captured via a screenshot and shared on a public website or social media account.

Understand what's happening behind your teen's apps and smartphone.

Facebook. This is the largest social network mostly made up of more parents than teens. But high school juniors and seniors start gravitating to Facebook as a way to stay in touch with family and also utilize Facebook groups for school activities such as cheerleading. A recent study shows 66% of teens use Facebook, essentially flat from 2015 when Pew Research Center data showed 71% of U.S. teens using the site.

Twitter. With 47% of teens using Twitter, this network is known as the real-time news network. Most teens have this account to follow YouTubers, sarcastic and humorous profiles, and celebrities, and girls tend to follow feminist-type accounts.

Instagram. The go-to app for all ages today, 76% of American teens age 13–17 use Instagram.

Tumblr. Fewer than 30% of American teens use Tumblr, Twitch, or LinkedIn. A heads-up on Tumblr, there is very little monitoring on porn and sexually explicit images and language.

TikTok. Forty one percent of TikTok users are aged between 16 and 24. In 2019 it was oneofhe fastest growingsocial networks pushing 500 million users. Teens use and abuse TikTok just like other apps playsfully, meanfully and sexually.

Snapchat. It seems low, but 75% of teens use Snapchat, or as I call it, SnapCrack. This mobile-only app offers the most dangerous ways for teens to get in trouble easily—and for trouble to easily find them.

LinkedIn. Known as the professional network, LinkedIn opened its membership to anyone who is 13 and older. This is the least used and by far the most beneficial network your teen can be active on when applying to college. It helps choose a college, get into a college, and can even help get internships. Above all, it creates a success-driven mindset and personal value that

Snapchat, Facebook, and Instagram do not. Bonus: LinkedIn influences your child's Google search results in a positive way. More tips here.

News Flash: Colleges don't count Snapchat streaks or Instagram likes as a marker of success or experience.
The good news with social media and teens is that it can be used as a portfolio for goodness, talent, and positive influence on society and community.

What can parents do to prepare teens for college and your child's social media footprint?

Do a Google search. I searched for my child's first and last name. What comes up in images? Or in the web results? I set up a Google Alert that notifies me any time my child's name is mentioned on the web.

Visit your kid's social media accounts. I went through all my teen's content. Is there profanity? Inappropriate images? Weapons? Here's a quick story on weapons: A rifle was found in the trunk of a high school student's car after posting about it on Twitter. It was shared across social media, including private Facebook groups. Your child might not be the one posting the original content, but if they share it with a supportive comment, this could be viewed as participating in illegal or inappropriate behavior.

Create a meaningful and purposeful content strategy that will help get your teen into college. My daughter volunteered this summer at a summer camp, I encouraged her to publish about her experience and set an example for others. Positivity versus sensationalism.

Look at their social media bios. Are they describing themselves in a positive and meaningful way? Social media is where personal branding starts at any age. I'm helping my teen use keywords that will help connect her positive characteristics, interests, and noteworthy accomplishments. For example, since my teen is on the cheer team and won state championships, I'll have her add that to the profile. Think valuable and meaningful versus meaningless.

Profile and cover images. Is it how you want your child to be portrayed by a college admissions board? Does it involve alcoholic beverages, questionable content, or provocative poses? Maybe an update is needed. For example, my daughter's college sorority doesn't allow any photos shared on social media involving alcoholic beverages.

Colleges and universities want your money. They want to accept your child as long as they meet today's standards and guidelines in a social media world. But the reality is they don't want to risk admitting a potential social media disaster that can tarnish the school's reputation.

It's our job as parents to guide our children in creating a positive social media footprint. Help them now before colleges reject them later—or worse.

···14···

Adulting the Steve Jobs Way

WHAT WOULD STEVE Jobs think about smartphone addiction today? After all, he started the craze in 2007 with the invention of the iPhone. If his vision was to make us never want to be able to put down our iPhone, mission accomplished.

Smartphone Addiction Symptoms

- Low Activity. Getting shit done becomes next to impossible

- Anxiety. The #FOMO (Fear of Missing Out) takes over your mind and body

- Withdrawal. Having a panic attack when your smartphone is not with you

- Intolerance. Getting annoyed when your smartphone time is interrupted

Today, we spend about five+ hours a day on our smartphone, doing just about everything from checking Facebook to banking to watching Netflix. Ironically making a call isn't even one of the most used functions on a smartphone. Instead, our smartphone addiction runs deep in mobile apps. Gaming is the most popular category next to business, education, and lifestyle. We're getting directions, listening to music, video chatting, and of course, feeding and grooming the social media monster.

The smartphone addiction causes are endless, with apps being the biggest lures. When Apple launched the App Store in 2008, it touted 552 apps. Today, we have 2.2 million apps available for download to choose from.

If you are wondering why you can't put your phone down, the struggle is real. It's actually called nomophobia, which means "fear of being without your mobile." And of course, there's an app for that. Time spent on mobile devices has almost doubled in the U.S. since 2012 and tripled in Brazil.

What's the big deal?

Twisted as it sounds, app developers are studying the brain and its response triggers. Why? They want to figure out exactly what it takes to push your brain cell buttons into tapping and scrolling your smartphone for as long and as much as possible. It's called brain hacking. I mean, after all, it's not the phone's fault, is it? Jobs didn't invent the iPhone so we would become co-dependent on it—did he? Maybe.

Staring at your phone is the new normal.

Gen Z is chatting on Snapchat. The Millennials are fantasizing on Instagram. Baby boomers are trolling Facebook. Gen Y and X are planning on Pinterest and job searching on LinkedIn.

Meanwhile, we're all dissecting the latest breaking news on Twitter. Also, if you work in in the social media marketing industry, there is no escaping the constant stream of notifications. In the background is Spotify while Fitbit is tracking your steps and reminding you to take a break. Hopefully, you switch gears to the meditation app that takes you away from your smartphone—mentally, at least.

The innovative genius and technological pioneer that he was, Jobs was also known for his deep spirituality. Everyone attending his funeral in 2010 was given a copy of his favorite book *Autobiography of a Yogi*. It was said to be his only book on his iPad and one that he reread once a year. Known for an infamous trip to India early in his career, Jobs credits the journey to helping him reinvent himself and giving him space to create a plan for the eventual rebirth of Apple.

What advice would Jobs give to us today about smartphone addiction? How would he feel about the possible distractions iPhones could be on his team?

The spiritual side of Jobs might give us these tips inspired by Yogananda, one of his favorite spiritual leaders:

Awareness

Smartphones can zap away our level of awareness. Walking and texting is a new talent—and dangerous, in case you missed the many YouTube videos of people caught texting and falling into fountains because they were not aware of their surroundings.

"Time is spent in rushing, in racing, in getting nowhere. Very few of us stop, think, and find out what life can give to us," said Yogananda in his writing on awareness. The modern-day message: slow down and stop trying to multitask.

"Every tomorrow is determined by every today."
Paramahansa Yogananda

Intention

What exactly are you trying to do each day? Get very clear on your intentions for the month, week, day, or hour. Your words, thoughts, and actions craft energy into your intention's outcome. Trying to write a book or article? Spending smartphone hours on your personal Facebook feed or Snapchat is not in line with your intentions. Neither is telling yourself you have writer's block.

> *"Since you alone are responsible for your thoughts, only you can change them."*
> *Paramahansa Yogananda*

Attention

Once you are clear on your attention, shift your attention to the things that will get it done. Try putting your smartphone on Do Not Disturb for a few hours each day so you can zero in your attention on your stated intention. When I realized my teenage daughter was up all night on Snapchat with her friends, I found an app for that. OurPact let me take control of her apps and shut them down at bedtime, the time when the intention was sleep.

> *"Opportunities in life come by creation, not by chance."*
> *Paramahansa Yogananda*

Productivity

Multitasking is not productive. The brain works best when there is focus, calmness, and breath. You get more done when you try to do less. Your smartphone can help increase productivity using one of the many apps, but it's a fine balance between using the productive side of your smartphone versus the time-sucking features that rob you of precious time.

> *"Don't do anything in a haphazard way; do everything with full attention, but don't do too many things. Pick up the more important things and do them with all your heart. Potentially, all knowledge is within you."* *Paramahansa Yogananda*

Sleep

Our smartphones are so smart they're even in charge of waking us up. But experts warn the blue light from a smartphone can have damaging effects on our sleep and can even cause cancer. Put the mobile device away at least two to three hours before going to sleep and read real books vs. ebooks in bed.

When you are in bed at night, try Yogananda's twenty body-part exercise, focusing on relaxation. Tense each individual body part with medium tension, then relax: left foot, right foot; left calf, right calf; left thigh, right thigh; left buttock, right buttock; abdomen, stomach; left forearm, right forearm; left upper arm, right upper arm; left chest, right chest; left neck, right neck; throat, back of neck. This exercise relaxes and also balances the inner energy flow, which might help you to be relaxed during sleep. No app required!

The reality of smartphone addiction: What would we do without them? It's our job to balance the poison and the power.

···15···

😫🩶

Space to Grieve

THAT MOMENT WHEN life changes forever. *Poof.*

Waking up on my birthday one beautiful Sunday morning, the mood changed pretty quickly when I read a breaking news alert on Twitter. A mass shooting happened in the middle of the night at the Pulse nightclub in downtown Orlando, Florida.

The number dead reached twenty then fifty. What? This was twenty minutes from our house, and these things just don't happen in Orlando. Well, now they do.

They happen in Orlando and pretty much across the globe anytime, anywhere. Just like that.

There are typically three major events that happen to us when life as we know it will never be the same. The events shape who we are and how we handle things. It's these events that influence our perception of the future based on the past.

We have predictable and manageable events such as starting a new school, moving to a new city, marriage, or having kids.

Then there's the unpredictable like our parents getting divorced, a sibling or parent dying suddenly, rape or sexual assault, bullying, or losing a child in an accident, to name a few harsh examples.

Then there are the extreme life events such as surviving a plane crash, making it out of one of the 9/11 towers alive, living through a natural disaster such as an earthquake, hurricane, or tornado, escaping a school shooting, or having one of your friends murdered by a serial killer.

Watching the Orlando mass shootings story unfold, it was hard not to get fully absorbed in the indirect heartache and pain that crushed a community and reached far beyond the Orlando city limits. Compartmentalizing like we can all do so well, my family and I still went about my birthday celebrations having brunch, sipping on mimosas and bloody marys, taking a boat ride to the sandbar, and soaking in the white sand, blue skies, and sunshine.

But the reality of social media feeds and live-streaming reports of the Orlando victims, friends, and family could not be avoided—and why should they be? This could happen to anyone, and we were lucky it wasn't us. Actually, I could relate because I once was one of those victims, family, and friends at a tragic point in my life. I could empathize for the other side of the screen of what they were going through. Shock, disbelief, numbness, and strength that comes from a space and place inside that you did not know existed.

My personal insights into grief, and the consequences of not allowing or giving yourself the space to grieve, go long and deep. My friends Tracy and Manny were murdered by a serial killer in the sleepy college town of Gainesville, Florida. Being the last to talk to Tracy and the first to alert her missing put me in the spotlight of one of the most horrific life-changing events in my early twenties. I *thought* I was grieving, but looking back, I was doing a really, really good job of compartmentalizing and being strong for everyone else. It's called survival mode, and I was good at it. If I only knew then what I know now about how important it is to give yourself space to grieve and recover.

What was supposed to be my week off in between jobs started with a very relaxing and lounging Monday morning watching Good Morning America. Then, a breaking news story. Two more bodies discovered murdered in Gainesville right next to the apartment complex where Tracy and Manny lived. After a series of frantic calls and 24 hours later, I soon discovered that they were the next victims of the monster terrorizing Gainesville and the University of Florida on what would have been the first day of school.

Calls, screams, confirmations, positive IDs, racing to tell parents before the media announced the names, camping out in their living room and front yard, keeping the hounding media at bay trying to interview everyone, attending two wakes in one day, and back-to-back funerals resulted in the saddest reunion of friends one could ever imagine, memorizing our high school's homecoming king and queen who had their lives tragically cut short when it was only just beginning.

I started a new job at a PR agency exactly one week after the murders, three days after the funerals, and in the midst of the manhunt trying to find the serial killer on campus. The details were unfathomable, and the fact that it happened to my friends was beyond comprehension. I still pushed forward and tried to go back to a *new normal* that would never really be normal again. I remember sitting in meetings with my new boss in physical and mental pain bordering exhaustion. Driving to see my first client, all I could think of was crawling into the fetal position, taking a nap, and fighting back tears of fear.

Fast forward to today, I can remember how hard it was to get dressed and out of the house that first day at work. My new boss told me not to worry if I needed more time off, she would understand. But I was so scared it would make me look weak or put me at risk of losing my new PR agency job that I said, "no problem" and showed up.

Big mistake.

Space and time will only allow you to heal if you give yourself space and time to grieve.

Throwing yourself into work, drugs, alcohol, a relationship, or a project without also letting in the healing and therapeutic space adds fuel to a fire that is sure to burn you out and spread you thin. I still remember what my therapist said to me when I complained that I was feeling like I was running on empty.

She said, "Honey, that's the first sign of depression."

Take time off, as much as makes sense, to give yourself the personal space to process, think, and restore in a healthy way.

Community

For indirect events that impact your daily life, such as a community tragedy:

- Give permission to leave; take a mental health day or hour

- Maybe it's as easy as reducing your work schedule that day

- Take a long lunch or leave work early

- Cancel unnecessary meetings that can wait a day or two

- Exhale. Go out and get some fresh air with a fifteen-minute walk

- Say no to more, say yes to less

- Pick up your kids early

- Surround yourself with friends and family

- Avoid going to your closest bar for comfort and remember that alcohol is a depressant that suppresses the reality and enhances the problems

- Find a yoga class or hit the gym for a change in perspective

- Find inspirational quotes to get you through the day and think happy thoughts like Holstee emails or Ralph Marston's daily motivation

- Create a Spotify song list to help get you through the day; research shows that listening to music can lift (or reinforce) your mood and ultimately lead to a greater quality of life

- Take five minutes every morning to have quiet time in your head to meditate and have silence with mobile apps such as Buddhify or Headspace

Direct Hit

If you (or someone you know) are hit directly with an extreme tragedy or life event that is sure to come with an abundance of grief, space might not be what they need.

Here is what I wish I knew then but do now.

- Take your mental health and happiness seriously by proactively getting help or getting someone help from a professional before there is an obvious problem.

- Attend every funeral. The close friends and family will always remember who shows up to their kids/parents/siblings, and it means so much to the immediate family.

- When something tragic happens to someone you know, don't be afraid to reach out and do or say something.
  - Here is the biggest myth: "Oh, I don't want to intrude when they want their privacy, or I don't know what to say."

- Messages, cards, texts, and phone calls letting them know you care and are there if you need them are extremely therapeutic and is the first of many steps in a grieving process.

- Take time out of your day to buy a card and mail it or send a private and personalized message via Facebook messenger.

- Just show up, unannounced is fine. People caught up in a tragic event in their lives don't return calls or ask for help—they need help.

- Breathe in suffering and breathe out the light of healing. Exhale with the Tonglen meditation practice: In times of distress and hardship, one visualizes taking in the suffering of oneself and of others on the in-breath, and on the out-breath giving recognition, compassion, and succor to all.

The Dalai Lama practices Tonglen every day and has this to say,

"Whether this meditation really helps others or not, it gives me peace of mind. Then I can be more effective, and the benefit is immense."

The less we respond to the negativity in our lives- the more peaceful it becomes.

Staying calm amidst the chaos is easier said than done. But with practice, such as disciplining yourself to stay in the pose when you want to give up, staying on your mat when the idea of leaving torments you in your ear, and just "being" when the pro-grammed neuropathways tell you that you need to deflect fidget, and react, you can retrain yourself to instead respond.

"It's not easy, but you're worth it."
  Kelly Green, owner of the Yoga Joint and Yoga Zen Master

···16···

The Six-Second Mind
Fix Test

THE LAW OF attraction works in mysterious ways, even six seconds. I first met Erin Pheil of MindFix during a mastermind
weekend. The only problem is we kept getting separated each
time we would strike up a conversation. Then we would run into
each other and get pulled away again and again. We'd just wave
each time we saw each other from a distance like BFFs at a big
party. The next week I received an envelope in the mail with
a one-of-a-kind envelope and old-fashioned handwritten letter.
Next you know we meet up on Zoom and find out Erin's digital
detox secrets to a mind fix.

So I could not help but share her magic.

Take this six-second test, and learn a secret about yourself no one's ever told you before.

Here's the test:

Complete this sentence:

What makes me important (or worthy) is _____.

For real.

Take six seconds, go back, and just finish that sentence.

I'll wait.

Done? Great.

Here's the secret I promised you:

If you filled in the blank with anything other than "nothing, I just am," it's almost certain that whatever you answered is actually a compulsion in your life, one that you struggle to stop yourself from doing even when you want to or know it's not in your best interest.

Here's what this looks like:

[working hard]

What makes me important is [working hard] → Hello, workaholic tendencies. (You likely often find it difficult to stop working, and if you're honest, will see that other parts of your life (relationships, free time, etc.) suffer because of how much you work.)

[achieving]

What makes me important is [achieving] → You win. Win. Win. But it's never enough. The day after an achievement, you're already focused on what's next. Next. NEXT. When you don't win/achieve anything for a period of time, you feel like shit. (Speaking from experience on this one.)

[taking care of others]

What makes me important is [taking care of others] → Sounds valiant, right? The thing is, you can't stop putting others' needs in front of your own. Everyone comes before you. You're okay only when you're supporting people and taking care of yourself or putting yourself first feels wrong.

[making lots of money]

What makes me important is [making lots of money] → You can't stop focusing on making more money. It's just never enough. The bar keeps getting raised.

[having others think highly of me]

What makes me important is [having others think highly of me] → You need praise from others. You feel awful when you don't get it. Criticism stings like hell. The possibility of rejection keeps you frozen.

The moment you say that your importance here on Planet Earth is a function of anything, you instantly teleport yourself to an eternally-draining hamster wheel of infinity with no end. (Because infinity has no end, duh.)

When your sense of worth depends on something outside you, you're forced to live out a vicious cycle of having to do [insert your answer from above]. Otherwise, you quickly begin to feel like you're not worthy or important. You quickly begin to feel like *shit*.

And that cycle repeats.

Until you die.

I'm not kidding.

It doesn't change on its own.

You can dull it, but it won't just go away.

As soon as [your answer above] doesn't happen, you begin to feel less okay.

When [your answer above] does happen, you feel okay about yourself, but only for the moment.

It's kind of like a getting a hit of a powerful drug.

If your self-worth is correlated to something that may (or may) not happen, your ability to be okay with yourself will always be in question.

I don't care how many inspirational quotes you read on your friends' Facebook feeds. Your answer to the test I above will override inspiration *every single time.*

What to do with this secret?

Watch it as it rears its head over the course of the rest of your month.

Watch how you feel about yourself when your [answer above] doesn't get met for a couple weeks.

Watch as you act compulsively—almost obsessively—to do [your answer above] at the cost of other important things in your life.

Watch as you see how difficult it is for you to act in any way contrary to [your answer above].

Observing a deep pattern like this in yourself is the very first step to breaking free of chronic self-doubt, self-criticism, and compulsive "I don't know why I can't stop" behaviors.

The After-Party

Catch up with Erin Pheil if you want more. She offers mental optimization consulting, website consulting, and free training. Follow her on Instagram and Facebook. @Erinpheil

...17...

Lisa's Favorite Digital Detox Secrets Apps

WE SPEND MORE than half our waking hours on digital. Given the data, it's impossible to think we will one day be digital free. The reality? Our lives depend on it in so many ways that we must figure out ways to make digital work for us and not against us. Over the years, I've made it a passion to curate apps that help align digital with improving health, wellness, and inspiration.

Mindful inspiration

Shine Text. This is a daily dose of positive affirmations, motivational quotes, and self-care actions you can take each day.

Jiyo. Ready to go from selfie to wellfie? Created by wellness expert Deepak Chopra, this is the one social network dedicated to your personal well-being. Some call it social media that actually matters, I call it the sanity network.

Aloe Bud App. *waiting to exhale* Looking for those nurturing self-care reminders and messages? Say hello to Aloe Bud app. You can customize it with your own schedule and reminders.

Work Focus

Brain.fm I love this app for getting shit done. You can choose between "Deep Work", "Creative", Study & Read", and Multi-Task" tracks depending on your mode. It's a gamechanger.

Meditation

Buddhify. This hidden gem is a combo meditation and mindfulness for the busy modern lifestyle. It comes with a beautiful user interface making it easy to pick a mediation for your mood and situation. My favorite tracks are sleep, waking up, and work break. These mostly guided meditations come with a soothing voice.

InsightTimer. With more than five million users, this one is perfect in addition to any other meditation app. (Why stop at one?) This free app also gives you access to a global community of meditators.

Calm. The name says it all. Who does not need an injection of Calm into their day? Soothing sounds of waterfalls, a crackling fireplace, or the ocean waves. Yes, please. In addition, this app comes packed with bedtimes stories, mediation tracks and challenges, and music and masterclasses on a variety of topics such as eating depression and happiness.

Headspace. Every day is a chance to train your mind for a happier, healthier life. Headspace is one of the most popular apps to help you do critical life things such as breathing, sleeping, and relaxing. It even has meditations for making the most out of walks, running, commuting, cycling, and vacations! Too young to meditate? Not possible. Headspace even has a meditation for kids.

Oprah and Deepak. 21-Day Meditation Experience. This superpower duo of spiritual wonderment is an experience not to be missed. Download this dynamic duo onto your smartphone and let the two superpowers of spirituality enlighten your soul.

Brain.fm Two tracks "guided' and "unguided" gives youthe power to control your mental state on demand using patented technology to elicit strong neural phase locking. Whatever it does, it works!

Yoga

Glo. When I'm on the road for work or pleasure and can't quite make it to a yoga studio, this is my go-to app. Besides yoga, you can also find meditation and thirteen styles of yoga, meditation, and Pilates, including vinyasa, kundalini, hatha, yin, restorative, and pre/postnatal. What I love most is that you can pick your duration, style, teacher, and level, and even focus on hormone balance, sleep, core, or digestion. There are forty-two types of focus, more than thirty body-part choices, and more than forty-five yoga instructors, including Sean Korn and Amy Ippoliti. You will have fourteen different yoga styles and levels one through three. Pick your time from five minutes to one hundred twenty minutes.

19 Minute Yoga. This app focuses on yoga classes in twenty minutes or less. It is designed to help you focus on the present and make better decisions using short, voice-guided classes so you can turn your attention inward and move with intention.

Fitness

Fitbit. I live by my Fitbit Blaze. I used to think that sitting all day at a computer was no big deal as long as I went to the gym or did yoga once a day. When I started tracking my movement—or lack of—I never realized how little I would actually move during the day. Having a Fitbit is a wake-up call to get up and get the blood moving in your body and brain. Tracking sleep, steps, calories, and weight make this a must-have for your lifestyle analytics.

MyFitnessPal. My husband and I lost twenty pounds each on a diet last year using MyFitnessPal. It helps figure out calorie counts and especially carb and fat when trying to stay on low-calorie and also low-carb diets such as keto or paleo.

#Digital Detox Secret

Check out Calm's masterclass called Social Media and Screen Addiction by Dr. Adam Alter, a psychologist who explores the who, what, when, where, and why of screen addiction. More importantly, he provides tools and actionable steps for managing social media and screen addiction.

#Digital Detox Secret

Have you experienced the moment when you're getting ready for a presentation, and suddenly the mind goes blank, your breath stops, and your nerves go into overdrive?

One of my favorite meditations on Buddhify is called "Ready" under the "Work." It uses a nano-technique called S-T-O-P. This eight-minute guided meditation gets you ready for your big moment with reminders to Smile, Touch, One Breath, and Pause. Slay your next moment, no Xanax required.

···18···

Lisa's Personal Digital Detox Secrets

OVER THE YEARS, I have created some favorites go-to's when it comes to self-care, self-love, diet, and nutrition hacks to a reset. Some are healthier than others. Not all of them are cheap, but there are budget-friendly versions so you can get creative.

Air. Get up and get out. Walking outside in fresh air is linked to lower rates of depression and is more effective than walking indoors. The increased oxygen to the brain improves clarity and function. Take fifteen minutes per day to walk in the fresh air.

Alcohol. No amount of alcohol is healthy, it is a gateway to other drugs and depression. Dr. Paul Savage says THC is by far healthier than alcohol. Don't get me wrong, I do enjoy my happy hours, just don't turn happy hour into every hour.

Ambien. If you want to end up like Celeste in *Big Little Lies*, sleep walking and driving, Ambien is probably not the best answer to getting more sleep. Check your hormones levels such as progesterone and testosterone and try things like melatonin and unplugging from digital.

Augmented Reality. AR is poised to help optimize our health and well-being in the not-so-distant future, making adopting a wellness lifestyle more convenient, easier to maintain consistency and accuracy, and helping make it more enjoyable whether you're a health nut or hate the idea of healthy living.

Baby Bathwater Institute. Skip the industry conferences. Join a mastermind community that's right for you with people who truly support you and care. It's all about the give. The keyword is community.

Baths. I take baths at night or any time I need a reset. Try CBD-infused bath bombs or a few drops on Ojai Energetics Hemp Elixir.

Beach walks. This is walking meditation.

Biohacking. Why not use cutting-edge technology, tools, and science–to become the best version of yourself? I follow BenGreenfieldFitness.com for all my biohacking digital detox secrets.

Bioidentical hormone therapy. Get your bloodwork done once a quarter to benchmark your hormone levels. Don't rely on your family doctor or OB-GYN; do your own research and go to a functional medicine doctor such as Dr. Paul Savage of Forum Health or Dr. Sangeeta Pati's Sajune Institute. Why?

"So much of the U.S. healthcare system is reactive," said Forum Health CEO Craig Weston. "Conventional medicine is built on an acute model. We deal with problems only after they happen—managing symptoms with pharmaceuticals and procedures. So often, this episodic approach to care falls short of addressing the true underlying issues."

Blowouts. Do what makes you feel good, look good, and saves time. For me, this includes blowouts. I can never get my hair to look like professional salon magic, so I bring my laptop and get a blowout before whenever I need to look good and feel good or better. Funerals, weddings, speaking gigs, conferences, interviews, big presentations, or date night.

Botox. I believe Botox reduces my stress levels and acts as an anti-aging strategy when used properly. Choose your doctor carefully, someone board-certified in cosmetic surgery like Dr. Paul Wigoda.

Brain.fm. Simply put, this app powers music designed for the brain (generated by its Artificial Inteligence) to enhance focus, meditation, naps, & sleep within 10-15 minutes of use. My productivity, sanity and mood are highly impacted on a daily basis thanks to Brain.fm

Burning Man. The ultimate digital detox. I have not been, but it's on my bucket list. Burning Man is a community, a temporary city, a global cultural movement based on 10 practical principles. It includes radical inclusion, gifting, radical self-reliance, radical self-expression, and immediacy.

Caffeine. I like the sound of *a triple grande skinny vanilla latte with whip*. Even though I am a big fan of Starbucks, the ingredients do not make me happy or healthy. For coffee from a company actually caring about the mind, body, and spirit, check out GetKion.com

CBD. It promotes healthy sleep, reduces anxiety and stress and keeps me focused and alert when I need it. Warning: CBD is everywhere. Make sure the CBD brand you are using is organic, full-spectrum, water-soluble and works in 30 seconds. Turn to trusted brands like the one I love Ojai Energetics.

Candles and salt lamps. My office and house are filled with calming and soothing lights. I hate fluorescent and bad lighting. While there is not much evidence to prove this, candles and salt lamps improve my mood, boost blood levels and raise energy levels, they do for me!

Deepak Chopra and Oprah Winfrey 21-day Meditations available at chopracentermeditation.com. Follow on Instagram at @deepakchopra for daily breath and infinite inspiration with deep passion.

Energy. They say time is our most valuable asset when actually our most valuable asset is energy. If we feel terrible, tired, stressed and toxic, time is useless. We need positive energy to make the most of our day. Eating whole foods, drinking lots of water, getting 8-10 hours of sleep and activating your body everyday will give you the energy you need to make the most of your time.

Essential oils. I use essential oils especially lavender for calming and peppermint for awakening. Mix the use of Ojai Energetics CBD hemp elixir with these essential oils for an instant mood changer. Natural compounds, like essential oils, have been shown to increase circulation and blood flow to the brain. I am a fan of Vibrant Blue Oils @vibrantblueoils

Facebook groups. Join a Facebook group that you can learn from and contribute to, even if they are paid memberships. It's a community-based way to use social media and not let social media use you.

Fiction. Close the self-help books and business books and escape from reality with a book like *Big Little Lies* or *Gone Girl.*

Hoarding. This is the inability to throw away possessions (including digital files, photos and clutter). Hoarding causes anxiety, stress and depression. Truth be told hoarding runs in my family. I am constantly getting rid of stuff and trying to stay organized and minimal. The podcast "the minamalists" podcast shows you how to live with less. Another source is Marie Kondo's book and her Netflix series Tidying. Her method helps clear out the clutter -- and choose joy.

Herbal Fiberblend. The most powerful and detoxifying cleanse. Scrub out your insides, get more energy, lose weight with a powerful combination of herbs and psyllium. I have been using this for more than 20 years. Read the reviews on Amazon before trying this so you have an idea what to expect. The results are worth it! A powerful colon cleanser that will sweep your system clean.

Hot yoga. The best detox; sweat out the impurities and stress. Did you know sweating in hot yoga is the equivalent of your body crying and provides psychological relief causing catharsis? Studies show that sweat and tears not only release the negative emotions, but they also release toxins, kill off 90 to 95% of bacteria in 5 to 10 minutes, and help improve vision.

Imposter syndrome. That "I'm not worthy" feeling. I've been there a million times. The first time I was asked to speak at a conference, I looked over my shoulder and thought they must have the wrong person. Maybe instead of Lisa Buyer they meant Lee Odden. When it was my turn to speak, I thought for sure someone would call me a fake and question my expertise. Ten years, a book, and hundreds of speaking events later, I feel the same way.

Imposter syndrome is something I didn't even know there was a term for until I joined the Baby Bathwater mastermind group of entrepreneurs and realized I was not alone. I always thought I was a very social person, but crowds actually stress me out. What do I do? Breathe. I also listen to the playlist on Buddhify app called "Ready" right before I'm presenting or doing an interview. It works. It's all in how you define yourself. You can also try a track from Brain.FM. I like the Chill track under Relax.

Some advice from Paleo Hacks co-owner and entrepreneur David Sinick after speaking at a mastermind event to a group of wildly successful business owners:

"I brought up my anxiety coming to this event and a lot of you spoke to me about it after talking about having similar feelings. It really drove home for me that we're all, for the most part, in the same boat. No matter what you're doing in your life, no matter how 'successful' you might be as a mover and shaker, we all still have that insecure teenager inside of us that's just trying to fit in and find their place in the world," he said.

Incense. Part of my daily ritual is burning incense when I wake up and sitting with just candlelight to start my day. It soothes my mental being.

Keto diet and intermittent fasting. Best way to stay lean and healthy and avoid toxicity and causes of inflammation.

Kombucha cocktails. If you are going to drink vodka, make it Tito's and kombucha.

Kundalini yoga. A secret weapon to clearing your mind and shifting perspective. It is an automatic brain shift. *You just need to make it through the first class.*

Marco Polo. This is a video communication app that helps you feel close, even when life gets busy. Millennial mom and digital marketing expert Virginia Nussey recommends this app to stay in touch with friends and family without having to be always connected.

Mental Health Days. When you are really stressed, tired, or feeling "off," take a mental health day.

Music. I am addicted in a good way to Brain.FM. My productivity, creativity, and focus are on high when I tune in. Download the app.

Necessary Losses. There are people you sometimes have to disconnect from, including family members or close friends. If they are not serving you, causing toxicity, or sucking the life out of you, break free and call it a necessary loss. This can be temporary or permanent.

Netflix. Escape the daily stresses of life using digital? Yes, it's possible. Best-selling author Aliza Licht and her husband turn to Netflix as a digital detox. Curl up on a weeknight with your favorite person and do a little binge watching. Disconnect from email, notifications and the likes of social media. Fall into another drama and out of your own. Some of my faves: Big Little Lies, Dead To Me and Frankie and Grace.

Off-the-grid vacations. Going places where there is no Wi-Fi or you are on a six to twelve-hour time zone difference. We went to Cuba for a family vacation and reconnected ourselves with each other and a new culture.

Paleo Hacks. This an insightful source for creative recipes, inspiration, and clean living. Paleohacks.com

Podcasts. Somehow, I got into listening to podcasts. Listen to one, host one, or be on one. Check out Wellness Mama podcast and my fave if you are an entrepreneur or digital marketer is Hustle and Flow Chart.

Prescription supplements. I take what my body is lacking, including Vitamin D. Don't buy over-the-counter, buy prescription-grade supplements.

Sleep. It is a superpower. I track my sleep using my Fitbit with a goal of an average of eight hours of sleep a night. I'm still working on this one! The OURA ring is a new wearable on the market winning over celebrity health entrepreneurs such as Dave Asprey is founder & CEO of Bulletproof and my friends at Baby Bathwater including the Wellness Agency owner, entrepreneur and investor Jay Faires.

"The metrics are tremendously meaningful and I can use them to make positive changes. The OURA gives you detailed information on your sleep states, heart rate, heart rate variability (stress level), body temperature, breathing rates, activity levels, and so much more," Asprey notes in his review on the Bulletproof website.

Spa days. I try to have a spa "office" day once a quarter or more. Massage, facials and a quiet space can do wonders for the brain, creativity and healing.

Sunsets. A way to take a break and find inspiration. Tip: You need to look up from your phone to see one.

Therapy. I have an official therapist and several unofficial therapists. Best investment ever. Note: Friends and family are not ideal therapists. Pay someone to give you objective and professional advice and support.

Time blocks. I try to keep my mornings to myself and not schedule any calls or meetings until after 1:00 p.m.

Virtual Reality. The next "big thing" like how social media changed our lives. I taught the first live yoga classes in Virtual

Reality on AltSpaceVR with evolvr.org. Grab a headset and see what you can immerse yourself in a new reality.

Vitamin D. One of the most well researched and clinically supported vitamins is bioidentical natural Vitamin D3. It supports calcium absorption and bone health. It also provides potential support for breast, cardiovascular, colon and immune health. The brand I use is MD Prescriptives.

Wine. I try not to drink wine every night. I'm still working on this one. :) There are proven health benefits of wine in moderation. We can justify anything. Check out the only health-focused, natural wine club—Dry Farm Wines—offering no sugar, keto-friendly, with no additives

Xanax. It's a great crutch and for sure has its merits when used properly, especially if you suffer from high stress and anxiety which can lead to burn out and then depression. Try a yoga class or meditation instead.

Conclusion

Be your true self.

Create space.

About the Author

Lisa Buyer is the author of Social PR Secrets in its 4th edition with a foreword by Guy Kawasaki. She is the CEO/founder of the Social PR agency The Buyer Group. She is also founder of FemaleDisruptors.com, a passion project with a mission to spotlight women who are disruptors in their space. Lisa is a member of Baby Bathwater and hosts a Podcast Digital Detox Secrets.

A certified yoga instructor, Lisa is a mom and wife She lives in Celebration, Florida with her husband and family. You can also find her on Anna Marie Island and Jupiter Beach, Florida part-time watching sunsets, going to yoga and working on her next business venture.

Follow her on digital
@LissBuyer
#DigitalDetoxSecrets

Made in the
USA
Columbia, SC